Habitat

Habitat

NEW AND SELECTED POEMS, 1965–2005

Brendan Galvin

LOUISIANA STATE UNIVERSITY PRESS

BATON ROUGE

Designer: Laura Roubique Gleason
Typeface: Minion text, Centaur display
Printer & Binder: Edwards Brothers, Inc.

Library of Congress Cataloging-in-Publication Data

Galvin, Brendan.
    Habitat : new and selected poems, 1965–2005 / Brendan Galvin.
        p.   cm.
    ISBN 0-8071-3046-x (alk. paper) — ISBN 0-8071-3047-8 (pbk. : alk.
paper)
    I. Title.
PS3557.A44H33 2004
811'.54—dc22

                                        2004022441

These poems have been selected from *Place Keepers* (Louisiana State
University Press, 2003); *The Strength of a Named Thing* (Louisiana State
University Press, 1999); *Sky and Island Light* (Louisiana State University
Press, 1997); *Saints in their Ox-Hide Boat* (Louisiana State University
Press, 1992); *Great Blue* (University of Illinois Press, 1990); *Wampanoag
Traveler* (Louisiana State University Press, 1989); *Winter Oysters*
(University of Georgia Press, 1983); *Atlantic Flyway* (University of
Georgia Press, 1980); *The Minutes No One Owns* (University of
Pittsburgh Press, 1977); and *No Time for Good Reasons* (University of
Pittsburgh Press, 1974).

Some of the new poems appear thanks to the editors of *Alaska Quarterly
Review, Crab Orchard Review, Crazyhorse, Gettysburg Review, Laurel
Review, Missouri Review, The New Republic, Sewanee Review, Shenandoah,*
and *The Southern Review.*

For our daughter Anne

Contents

New Poems

Place Keepers (2003)

The Strength of a Named Thing (1999)

Sky and Island Light (1997)

Habitat

New Poems

Fogdog

Barely a light at all,
and seemingly without source,
a fogdog comes one or none to a fogbank,
not a small deposit
the sun makes, but otherworldly pale
as a candle held aloft in a house
floated across this bay
from Long Point or Billingsgate
two centuries ago, as if where droplets
and damps are working on shingles
and fascia boards in these
soft November days
someone were searching yet.

I could say this place
has been storied into meaning
by its humans, but these phenomena
are not metaphors: there's a twisted
delta class magnetic field
above sunspot 9715
that's going to cause explosions
up there, and send gusts of solar wind
toward us around the first of next week.

A fogdog this morning
where the river at full moon
invades the flats back of Egg Island,
and a few days after the Leonid meteor storm
briefly connected all the dots,
a black cloud drove a rainbow before it
as I came to the top of Tom's Hill—
that moving spectrum another first
in my weather annals.

Things out here on the edge
are traveling with their mysteries again.
Yesterday while I worried these events
the wind unleashed an answer
miles away down the beach and sent it

leaping like a tumbleweed over
washed-up obstacles
to come whicketing past me
as a plastic bucket,
a cracked yellow human construct
churning out groans as it went.

Catboat

Year upon year, trial and error:
of a thousand anonymous quahoggers
looking up from low tides, rubbing their backs,
one studying his widow-maker
anchored in the mud is thinking,

Push the width toward the stern
so her beam's half her length
and you've got a broader, flatter deck,
less chance of going ass up.

Then another, scratching the flats
miles and years away: Maybe shove
the mast up closer to her bow and hang
a longer boom for more canvas.
You've got storage up front then—add
a low cabin—and the load's
that much closer to the keel.

The way an idea is layered, her keel's
laid on in strips of fir. Red cedar
lengths, an inch square, bend
to the fit from bow to transom,
until she's like a horseshoe that will float.

Above a lifesize blueprint called a lofting,
form is following function now
and forever. When it comes to workboats,
this is one of the shapes necessity evolved,

broad-beamed but shallow,
almost a scallop shell for the hummocks
and shoals of these northern waters,
but stable around the holes and channels,

her one large sail laid on for speed upwind
and down, and to come about
quick when water and sky turn ugly,
and get you to hell home.

A Few Local Names of the
Double-Crested Cormorant

This is the fishbird that flew here
directly out of its fossil imprint, unchanged
for sixty million years, hell's turkey
from its punk hairdo to its black rubber
scuba-flipper feet, hanging its wingspread
to dry on rocks and creek banks, crosstrees
of masts, the insignia of a country that has
no plans for peace and no word for civility,
nesting in branches of matted seaweed
this guano goose fixes in a mixture
of its own trashfish paste and pellets,
until the tree surrenders of chagrin
and collapses to poison its pond. It is all
overstatement, stink duck and goo loon,
and can make a buffet of a fish farmer's
ponds, then slime every deck in the harbor
with the by-product overnight, collateral
damage, its green mineral eyechip
and yellow gawp testimony that it knows
it has thrived beyond dinosaurs
and will slip past even the cockroaches
on its own slicks, this gluebird,
stool pigeon, shag rat.

For the Raven's Return

I keep checking out the North Pamet crows
for the Great Corvid who may slip into town
and wear that whole flock for his cloak.
I'll know him by his diamond-shaped tail
and the way he flies upside down, aerialist
above winter, the envy of grounded herons
puffed up against that gulag weather.

Raffish and disreputable, those old mariners
who lurch on the slippery cobbles in my sleep
understand and speak all sixty-four
variations of the quork to companion
ravens riding their shoulders.
That's how they keep those eyebright
hunters sitting there, ruffed out in blue-green
and warbling to themselves for an hour at a time
like introspective drunks.

Korax the Croaker should be welcomed this way,
those sailors tell me:
                        Out of everything
eastbound from Long Gone, bears on the beltway,
that moose on the library lawn, cougars, coyotes,
fishers, it's you we need most, whom no supervisor asks,
Why did you do it this way and not that way? Why were you
there yesterday when you should have been here?

From gilded perches in the capitols, our representatives
sing the lobbyists' tunes. Bring your reclusive talents
and replenish us with all you have learned in exile, Croaker,
for the steeple-crowned hats that ratified
your old-world repute and drove you out of here
have gone west themselves, and the roadkills
multiply, tributes and honoraria for you:
full moon raccoons, skunk courtships thwarted by
our Interstates in the first week of February.

Make of these trees taking our cornfields back
your great hall again. Dumpsters multiply

for you across the land; inside the hollow steeples
of churches, the cell phone towers grow taller,
reaching for that year when no one will stand
in silence alone without punching the numbers in,
when no one will hanker to crack their wings
and fly around cronking.

Hummer

A few feet away in fuchsia,
wings are inferred.
She signs the air with herself
so fast the whole benediction
is visible, then gone,

& when I look around she sits
resting on the line among plastic
clothes-pins—synecdoche,
metaphor, or just a sense of humor?

Air's ampersands, seahorses
of the aether, Thomas Morton believed
they live on bees, & Loranzo Newcomb,
thinking to taste their nurture, went about
inhaling the essence of trumpetvines.

This one's an ounce emphasizing
the grossness of chickadees,
hinting at the design of the Concorde
that used to boom out over the Atlantic
each morning around 8:30,

& so quick she has few
effective enemies. If extremes
truly contain their opposites,
she & I have at least
that in common, along with
a life among the trees.

Riffing Deciduous

Summer, old bore, though we love the ways
　　you reduce everything to five shades
　　　　of green, one of these days

in a fall of soft tonnage, your stranglehold
　　on the obvious must end. We need those
　　　　deciduous farewells that reveal

from cranberry bog to hogsback,
　　from seagrass to sky at dusk, not red
　　　　but its modulations: solferino, murrey,

minium, not yellow but vitelline and those
　　others nameless as the obscurer insects.
　　　　On one of those clarified mornings,

in a nest like a straw handbag
　　hung to the weather, in a fright wig out on a limb,
　　　　in cones of grass and false beards

precariously woven, the instinctive faith
　　of birds will reveal itself to a walker's eye.
　　　　As if to prove all things must have their time,

the textures of fox sparrows will be
　　no longer subtle, but flashy and necessary,
　　　　until we can trust that if we pay attention

we'll hear the groaning into being
　　of things believed in though unseen—a gasp
　　　　as chives gain the air, and even before equinox

the sound of a rubbed balloon
　　as wings chafe cold from the winter-brittle blue.

Dogs of Truro

The first anonymous baying
from those backlit hills petitions a single
greeny-blue winter star.
It silvers as I watch, tuning its sharpness.
Deep January in the natural dark,
and now another to the south is yelping,
Sladesville trying to talk with Prince Valley,
or Corn Hill calling Pond Village across
the cold. This is their time, who have
no heaven unless they create it
with their fierce singing from hogsbacks
and down in the evergreen-lined
pockets of the dark. At such ululating,
even the sea hushes and the landscape
turns black and silver—a negative of the day.
This one now may be saying, I am Magnus
of Crow Hill, and here is my story, or Lilith
from Castle Road may be claiming she raised
that moon that's just clearing the trees
toward Ballston. Later the owls will take over,
as by woodstoves and under coffee tables
these yodelers and wailers run their legs
in dreams, but it's sociable for the moment,
contact, contact, a whisker tickling
a crystal of frost, the stars drawing nearer,
a planet turning to listen.

A Buck's Prints in Winter

Three weeks after deer season, and except for
an orange flareup in the woodstove's window,
the hoard of protective coloring is gone,
even that hunter's gone who waited with
Death's patience in leaf fall
and shadow of Gore-Tex on Bald Hill
over there, arrow notched, his bow
engineered to drive a steel tip through cement.
Another human season survived, and this buck's track
is stamped like three-inch broken hearts
in roadside sand again. He has run coyote gauntlets
from the high pines all the way down to the river,
though nightly now that pack
petitions the hunter Orion with faltering cries
I picture flattening out like woodsmoke on the air.
But the murder on my mind's another
Sunday-night-movie plot: sex, sad choices,
and money, that left a toddler
crawling a bloody floor and brought
the media ponies to town,
flexing their famous hair and backing us
to the wall with microphones, getting it all wrong
until the body and the story cooled,
all of it irreconcilable with that buck I've watched
drinking in the river, tutelary spirit
of a rain-fogged afternoon, and startled
sweeping downhill as I went to the woodpile,
antlered ghost crashing through brittle reeds,
cattails he burst in passing out of sight
the puffs I thought were gunsmoke.

Blues for a Kettle Pond

Each June we carried that year's carpentered raft
on our shoulders the mile from home, going barefoot
like holy pilgrims over the nobbled oak roots
on those hot sandtracks,

passing Rollie Wilson's dragger slowly oxidizing
in his yard even as he rigged her for a season
of scalloping that never seemed to arrive.

Then on rails blue as oil with the heat
we'd leave a few cents for the Tuesday or Thursday freight
to flatten,
          a bomber out of Otis droning over,
trawling its red sleeve toward ack-ack practice
down the peninsula.

               Where the road halved
to a downhill path through mixed pine forest and oak,
wintergreen grew wild in the shade on both sides,

and strong enough to keep on your tongue until
it summoned an apparition of water among the trees.

Kids who swim themselves blue-lipped
and prune-fingered there now must believe
in all innocence they own that kettle pond

to its white-sanded depths, but to get there on that old
true road to memory's Compostela
they'd have to lift a cobbled raft off the ground

and work its bent-nailed corners through the new
tenters' village populous as any bivouac,
and on into kitchens where the dishwashers

downshift through cycles for women in designer
Hopi gear and their men in the happy whites
of Manhattan fieldhands, lives slick
as magazine covers,

                    then on past
a greenhouse where a man eats late dinners
alone by candlelight, like a troll trapped
in a block of remnant ice,
                              its chilling wisps
curled up under whatever pines
may be left now, the last of a glacial block
rumored still to be down there,

the source of cold you'd feel when you listened
to the muffled rote of surf-splash from over
a northeast hill and the dunes beyond until,
with a sudden pulse-tremor like a fish taking flight,

the air would quell in those high pines. That shore
is torn with the riprap patterns of all-terrain tires now,
and I have looked everywhere for a pond
whose water rests as mildly as then.

A Gift Apple from Derry, New Hampshire

for Sarah and Rod

This time when he showed up in my dreamlife
the night air had an edge to it,
a tang some apple trees were brewing.
He was not so much America's foxy
grandpa as a classical shade offering
a yellow-green fruit, telling how
a vein opened in him
as crooked and black as any line
he ever drove across a page,

and beneath him love's
tectonic faults kept shifting while
he learned from that young orchard
that a fine thing needs patience
as well as pruning, measures taken
to distribute the load.

As a way of supporting poetry
he tried to grow Gravensteins like the one
in his hand, he said, a September bearer,
and the other cash crop fruit,
Baldwins and Northern Spies, late
and hardy for wintering over.

Though the deaths of his children
gathered before and behind him
like surrounding woods at dusk,
he went deeply into those thirty acres,
made them his own, saw that he'd
never get to the bottom of them.

Sir, I asked, *when this apple
has puckered in a desk drawer,
what will I have of yours?*
Measures to untangle the mystery
from misery, he said, to give yourself
more spring and breathing room.

Blackthorn and Ash

CARNDONAGH, DONEGAL

Doherty's cows are staring from the next field
in hopes of a rough lick of salt off our palms,
and we are staring at a few tumbled walls,
not even thatched sheds now, slick with
the morning softness off Trawbreaga Bay—
Bryan and Bridget's farmstead in Ballyloskey,
themselves a hundred years in the churchyard
a mile below, among the Tolands and Divers
and Dohertys. So this is the source,
obscured by the ash trees and blackthorns
growing through rooms my grandfather's
mother and father grew their children in,
before the boys caught rides to Moville and took
the lighter out to the Glasgow-Boston steamer
anchored on Lough Foyle, with ash twigs
in their pockets, charms against drowning,
that tree possessing the power resident in water.
Straight as the heart for hayforks and oars, too,
but flexible for the ribbing of curraghs,
and possessed by a poetry of its own:
wind on the deep, moon of the waters, it linked
the inner and outer worlds, clearing the way
of strife. Which would be the precinct
of blackthorn, that strife, wood of the clubs
of faction fighters, its sloe fruit a pucker for satire,
for latter-day Vikings around a kitchen table,
in for teatime off Loughs Foyle and Swilly
and pressing a crown of those thorns to one
absent forehead or another. Blackthorn and ash,
balanced somehow in those children I remember
white-haired at wakes in their dark suits.

The History of My Hat

To keep the rain and wind off my skull
I needed a hat of bawneen, that miracle fiber wool
not far enough from the sheep to have lost
its smell of origins and natural waterproofing,
wool any sailor can tell you is more than mortal,
and gray as those rocky jags on Doagh Island
that lean north, pointing the way the glacier went,
though textured too with a black and white stubble
rough enough to support the blackberry stitch
and suggest that fruit's beard and its thorny
brambles that lash back at wind and rain
in the waste places where it thrives. But I needed
a moss stitch, too, since that plant flourishes
where mists hang low and regular, and a trellis
pattern like fields fenced with the stones
lifted from them, to remind me how I came
from Ballyloskey. Oh, and a honeycomb pattern
to induce the sun and remind the bees
they have work to do far from my person.

A Neolithic Meditation

NEWGRANGE

They'd have handed you a hide sack
and a cow's shoulderblade to shovel with
here, and sentenced you to daily quotas
from the gravel pit or a sod-field
past its prime, or with better luck, to paddling
a dugout down the Boyne where that salmon
and its wisdom was always beyond
the spearhead. Out of the overseer's eye
you'd be able to pace yourself until
you returned with a boatload of white stone
for enhancing this burial mound's face.
Full of noose-around-the-neck wisecracks,
you'd have been an unwilling toiler,
envying the horse its stamina,
the hare its jagged speed over broken
fields, and bog cotton its deference to wind
on peatlands against blue mountains,
where it crowds white-headed
as ancient peasants herded off the best
grazing, enduring as if they'd do better
as plants hoarding minerals through winter,
hairy prodigals spinning existence from clouds,
from mistfall two days out of three, the odd
shoal of sun drifting across. If you've come here
for your roots, lay an ear at grazing level,
down where even the sheep-splats
awry on stones are beginning to raise moss,
the level of folk wisdom, where maybe
you'll hear, "Need teaches a plan,"
or "Better to live unknown to the law."

Mouth Music

They call me Eugene Maher in Ballyconeely,
if I deign to stop that way on my road at all.
In Fahan they say I'm Owen Doherty,

who is thicker by half and feet taller than me,
but that's no bother. It's just as logical
to say I'm Eugene Maher in Ballyconeely—

where every friendly doorknob gives me entry
to a plate groaning at the high table—
as to call me whozits—Owen Doherty,

your only man in Fahan for a party.
There are places they call me Eamonn MacGunnigal,
but they call me Eugene Maher in Ballyconeely,

only because I am too ragged and wee
to be taken thereabouts for James Ross Gill,
and nobody in Fahan calls me McIlhenny.

Guess my proper name and your pints are free.
You'll be the toastmaster of Donegal.
A hint: In Muff when I claim I'm Mickey Sweeney,
they send the boy around for Dr. Healy.

A Woman at Lake Pontchartrain Park

Somehow the sky this morning
got under a far shrimper and lifted it
off the water, nets and hull, and turned
the North Shore to floating blue islands.

Hillingar Effect: the cloudless air
stills and stabilizes over a cooler surface
and curves light to a lens that elevates
distant images above the horizon,

a wonder lost on this woman who's sitting
among motley vans and the parti-colored cars
of those who seem to be living on the road.

All day behind the Volvo's wheel, facing
the levee that keeps the lake from a suburb,
she has watched as if someone
with the directions might walk over its ridge.

Something has ended for her. She looks
crammed in with the plaid suitcases
and stuffed garbage bags. Now at her back
a race is in progress, an afternoon

of bright spinnakers behind the gray slick
of trouble on her face: miles out on the lake,
they may only remind her of empty
detergent bottles bobbing on the waves.

And these palm trees, the fish crows and pelicans?
This black flock of jumpy, water-walking coots
with their white beaks—even those glossy
ibises hunting bayou sloughs on the road here

must be lost on her. Fed up or thrown out,
she has gotten only this far from the rupture
of routine. Here where no being with wings
or suspension of gravity
can touch her isolation clear as starlight.

Byrum Between the Headphones

Sweeping my Bounty Hunter over the sands,
I'm an outrider of the tendency for small
shiny things to drift, a shepherd
of random slippage who thanks God for gravity
every summer morning I'm out here
with sun gilding the tide—one of
the finer things in life.
                            Before even the earliest
beachrats arrive with today's losses,
sometimes a watch, sometimes a set of keys,
gold earring or pin, I'm on the case
for yesterday's accidents. I don't turn up my nose
at dimes and quarters either, whatever
puts the frosting on my Navy pension.

Better this than mowing lawns
for the summer complaints. That's for
a couple of other vets, with my blessings:
just give those homeowners the leisure
to get down here to the beach and begin
losing things, and I'm my own boss.

It would almost make you a philosopher,
some of the things you find. A locket
with a picture of a dog? A pair of handcuffs
inscribed, *Love is not love which alters
when it alteration finds.* I mean,
what does that mean?

Since I'm no car thief or housebreaker,
the keys I drop in parking lot trash barrels,
the watches go to a jeweler in Hyannis
who has asked not to be named, but the metal
I sell to Harold Kelsey, who melts it
to new pins and earrings for his shop,
stuff that looks like miniature roadkills,
but that's his business, not mine.

                   Mine yields
best from beaches the headshrinkers frequent.
Amazing all they drop, lose, forget
or leave behind, although an upholsterer
showed me a leather easy chair once
that he had into the shop pretty regular,
belonged to a shrink who kept falling asleep
and burning holes in the arms
with cigarettes . . .
                   That's how I came by
this Rolex here. Some doctor. It's mine now,
Law of the Sea. All but the monogram
JLS, MD. I'm thinking of changing my name
to John L. Smith, Doctor of Medicine.

Ploesti

When they trapped my uncle Red McHugh
in a corner of the corridor, he grabbed
the vacuum cleaner wand from a custodian
and held three or four attendants off,
poking them with it, trying to suck the shirts
off their backs. Same with the two cops,
everyone trying to reason with him
above the keening vacuum while
the front desk phoned my cousin Ruthie.
I was locked in traffic on route 128
when she buzzed me: "Can you get over
to Pine Shores Pavilion? They've thrown
my father out, can you believe it? Seventy-five
and evicted from an elderly facility?"

An hour-and-a-half later he was outside
on a lawnchair, all attitude and packed bags,
red flesh still tight to the bone, his silvered-over
scars looking like tribal markings, reminding me
how as a kid I'd watch him trying to shave
around Frankensteinian lines of stitches
in the steamy bathroom, more than once
his head bandaged like a turban.

Attendants stood at the rest home doors,
even the windows, watching us load the car,
their arms folded like eunuchs in a Fifties
harem flick. Cowboy Red McHugh—
he'd brought the name upon himself
as a patrolman:
                    trapped a housebreaker
in an attic steamer trunk and put one through
a protruding hand when the perp wouldn't come out
on his own; jerked unrepentent speeders
through car windows; forced a truck full of hot furs
into a lake with his cruiser, and somehow
or other made captain.
                    "They had me in a room

with a whistler. Whistled through his teeth all day,
looking out the window like he was planning
an escape, but alls he had in mind was whistling,
so I coldconked him.
                              The whole week in there
revolves around this twinkie showing up
to diddle the organ in the Residents' Lounge,
Friday afternoon sing-alongs. I'd rather go back
to Ploesti."
                    "What's Plusky's?"
                                        "How soon
they forget," he said, and looked at me
like I was something that crawled
into the car through an air vent.

"A Nazi oilfield in Rumania. We bombed it,
made our run so low the blasts
drove all this cornfield chaff right up into
the bomb bay. On the way back to North Africa
I was sweeping it into the Mediterranean Sea.
You've heard of that, right?
We didn't know until after the war
only one out of three of all those B-24s
made it home. Flying coffins. Came in so low
I can still see the look on a German kid's face
as he fell away from the machinegun
he was firing out a window. A little riper,
we'd have had a fuselage full of popcorn.
No way I end up rooming with a whistler.
I'd rather go back again and bomb Ploesti."

A Footnote to Power

On a day so still you might think
that saying *wind* out loud
could start a crack the equinox
would ooze golden from,
I found a bolt on Corn Hill Road,

and weighed it in my hand,
feeling its otherworldly cold,
as though it had dropped
from the undercarriage of a cloud,

and listened to the nuthatch
telegraph in bushes whose maroon haze
signified their readiness
to begin again, a few natural egg cups
woven in them here and there,
abandoned but waiting.

Thick as my thumb and longer
than any teacup-sized warbler's nest
is deep, that heavy-duty piece
had an octagonal head on it

larger than any resting place
a hummingbird might bind
to the merest knuckle
of an apple tree, a steel bolt shaken
to unthreading, and fallen.

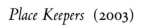

Place Keepers (2003)

May Day

for Ellen

Suddenly tugged from behind, the work
of an oriole, one spray of the apple tree's
floweration is trembling, looking the way
it feels when a fish begins nibbling
your line. Isolations of nuthatch
and chickadee are slowly giving way, warming
into affinities. It began a month ago:
goldfinches blew into the pussywillows
and swung on the stems until we saw
that the uppermost catkins
had already sprung their bee fuzz.
Think of Catesby sketching a treefrog
clinging to the New World's
skunk cabbage, or his buffalo of the woods
engaging an itch with a bristly
locust tree: those juxtapositions,
like you and me, that prove it takes
two of anything for something to happen.

Cold Water Elegy

The old boatwright Avery Bearse is dead
again, and it's your turn
to build the skiff. A gray outport
on a stony coast, with skies the color
of wharf shacks. The tools on your list
will be coming by late bus: fishtail
gouge, bench dog, dovetail jig,
bullstone. It isn't those that get you,
but the sad-sounding ones Avery
knew by hand, froe and scarp,
fretsaw like something you might coax
a threnody with. Worse are the tools
you have no idea about, the rifflers
and eye punches, inshaves, trammel-heads.
This dream of yours is a lot like that joke
the Shingler pulled when you were a kid
and roofing the Outermost Motel: Go over
and ask Arkie Johnson can you borrow
his funk chunker. Except that you
have to get Avery Bearse to that island
on the oyster-colored edge out there,
before it wears thinner than curtain lace.
Valsay it's called, and in some places Fulva.
Another Celtic take on the world's
footlessness, last week it was spotted
off the coast of Sollay: a sudden calenture
or trick of light where the sea
should be open all the way to Canada.
And now cloud shadow creeps
across those slopes. The wind downshifts
on the road from Baffinland. You stand with
your list at what those mean laughers inside
claim is the bus stop, under a lamp
the bugs won't visit for another seven months.
Trying to find a way to deliver Avery Bearse
to the other side of cold water, all you can think

is how this life is a lot like your mother's
old lament: First they tell you
you've got the wrong screwdriver, then
they say you've got the wrong screw.

The Blue Island Log of Herman Gill

Sepias of an old winter: a man standing
full height under a berg like a grotto
deposited on the beach, behind him
the marshes a frieze of no color,
spiky with terrors, and a northwest wind
you can almost hear in the photo.

He is Herman Gill, keeper of Blue Island
Lighthouse. After months of winter,
he has logged how snowy owls
have drifted down to float crisscross in
spook flights before the beam of his great light,
and how they refuel their yellow eyes
on the wild offspring of his children's rabbits.

All night his bachelor quarters complain
around the stove. One morning
along his beach route he came upon
a white owl untying the mysteries of a cod,
and more fish sealed in a slab of ice
nearby, like sequinned slippers.

Watched by snow, he has learned to look
about him for a pair of gold eyes,
and has minted a weather saw for his logbook:
a white owl in November
means weather you'll remember.

This morning, March 14, he wrote,
Brushing soot from the cold flue ledge, I touched
a thing so soft—a finch, I saw by its beak,
with feathers now gray as a catbird's
from beating long in the chimney
it had entered to get out of the wind.

It died in a blind shiver behind the stove
as I wondered was it the same bird
that beat on the light's windows,
golden in that glare one night, wings
a transparent yellow, lost, confused,

then swept away, the glass reading
twenty-seven, the windspeed fifty-four—
so I thought of Cora and the children,
and our house flaked to a puzzle
by the Doane Brothers and barged
to the mainland for reassembly.

Here there are days so empty of speech
I believe I could detect the sound
light makes as it creaks around toward
equinox, even hear the pop
of Cora's daffodil leaves
taking their explosive stance about
the imminent flower.

But then I open the door to find
only wind bushing around the walls,
and one morning the passing
crew of the *Hannah Rich*, waving on deck
as though reprieved of mortal duty,
a joyride of breaking ice
that kept them and left for the horizon.

Holdouts

A quick flurry of snow buntings
flocking here and there above
the dunes and marsh grass,
and remnant sanderlings, brant,
horned larks, such spectacle
I would have tripped over that
thing spotted like the wrack line
had I not heard it crooning
to itself and seen the flipper
wave as though it was orating
or working out whether
to slough a skin and walk into town,
giving someone seven years of joy
before a lifetime of trouble
and a patrimony for the books.
Hauled out on the beach
it might have been any sun lover
waiting on its back for July,
off guard and unaware because
nobody's standing here in the wind
these bottom months, only me.
It raised a face round-eyed
and whiskered, a cartoon uncle's
caught in the act, though the retreat
into its element was almost casual,
a slow-motion sack race.
Then those eyes were drawn
to shrewdness under heavy brows,
the skull a helmet, olive drab—
one of the seal folk was studying
a man hauled out of his routine
and relating some grievance to the sea.

2. *The Bones*

They are brown here in the lee
of Gull Island, like old wood
carved and sanded.
                     The tide
that visits them strips away veneer
so they look shipped across time
as well as water,
                     and yet I want to say
I knew the harbor seal whose flesh
contained them as its instrument.

Last winter there were times
it fled the riverbank, a shadow
in the current, then a face

breaking from the flow, as eye to eye
we checked each other out.

Eyes are the first to go in the lee
of Gull Island, and then the face. Fallen
things are not long in the flesh here,

but this has left a harp or lute,
medieval, to fit between a hand
and clavicle, or balance on a knee.

It has a neck, a fingerboard and frets—
a forty-stringed sarangi, perhaps,
unstrung now, or else a koto or tarab,

tuned with these pegs and keys,
something a bow or plectrum
drew music from, which now is elegy.

The Gang from Ballyloskey

Some mornings, missing the feel of lather
and the blade, one of those Ballyloskey farmers
creeps into my mirror for a second,
face like a woodknot with blue eyes.
Sometimes in wind I can almost
hear them rooting for me, all the dead
from Ballyloskey, point of origin:
eternity as spectator sport.
That human compost pushed me out
into this vale of duffers and fumblers,
and may one day take me back, but for now
they watch the moves of everybody
they've passed their looks and lights to,
making the side bets and the accusations:
He got that attitude from you folk. And why
shouldn't the dead enjoy us? It's more fun
than harping on forever, a lot less dangerous
than Valhalla. Today they may be saying,
He's only scratching with a pen. Let's see
what his cousin the police chief is up to.
Sometimes a flash off a store window
gives me a few faces in passing, ditch-beards,
pie-eyed color commentators, a lineup
of root vegetables, nobody too far
off the ground. Behind them the mountain
is laced with stone walls, there's a celtic cross
or two, and hard by a jar of plastic flowers,
a jug of the right stuff, then the whole
graveyard swept with cloud.

The South Uist Bus

(OUTER HEBRIDES)

He's a wee handy man, climbing
onto the bumper to whack the battery
into compliance with a stilson.
Now the little green bus turns over and begins
to lurch forward, and he settles it
into fifteen miles an hour. "A quarter
of a million on her," he says,
"and good for another." It's him and me,
and I'm here for the *machair*,
twenty miles of buttercups, orchids, vetch
and birdsfoot trefoil exuding a yellow haze
that floats just above the ground
the whole western length of the island,
the Atlantic beyond through lapses of dune.
Greenshank country, with snipe signing
the air in random whistling zig-zags,
lapwings, redshanks, oystercatchers,
and the ruins of a second-century
wheelhouse at Kilphedar. He's here
because somebody in Ulster an eon ago
got tired of dodging Niall of the Nine Hostages
or his like, and rowed over one night
to discover fishing and farming
were more congenial to a long life.
One eye's on the road, one's studying
my rucksack and seventeen-pocket parka,
and he's no doubt wondering why anyone
would go into the *machair* except
to pasture cows. "Have a care if you get
up island," he says. "The army may be
banging about on their missile range
today. Ach, I've sailed merchant marine
around the world, and they hate
the English everywhere." He'll stop
for anyone who can raise a hand,
at Howmore, by the corner of the road

to Ormaclete, near a house
glued all over with starbursts
of purple mussels and scallop shells,
"I'll be along" his only schedule.
They're old women mostly, heading off
for lochside houses, and one ancient couple,
joined by the handles of a plastic grocery bag,
all of them speaking "the Garlic,"
weather talk I'm guessing. "A hen harrier!"
I must have just shouted it, because I'm
the one pointing. And I'm the foolish one
when he wrestles the steering wheel
and pulls the bus over so I can take in
the silver male hawk circling the bog
and they can take me in, all of them smiling,
pleased I've come all the way from America
to admire their island, or else this
is how they handle the mad. The bird
sails off east toward the mountains.
"Thank you," I say to no one
and everyone, and back on the road
they're smiling and nodding at me,
speaking that poetry of conspirators,
and our driver says, "One of us
wants to know where a man
might buy a pair of boots like those."

Listening to the Courtship Delirium of the Great Horned Owls

Nightly now, under the Snow Moon,
they are singing of Love as they understand it—
that big ticket item that leaves us tongue-tied.
So their offspring will land with roof-thumps
over our heads, come next May, they sing it
as they were meant to, *basso profundo*
in moonwhite that magnifies leaf scutter,

for no reason at all recalling how,
in Dingle once, I stepped from a phone booth
into a swirl of long-stemmed bridesmaids
debouching from cars—O attar of petals,
dangerous pastels—and, shrunk to crocus height,
I was willing to be that tall forever.

So what if some critical strain of eighteen-wheeler
rips through these moments? That's what I asked the dark
last night when the owls woke me. So what if it happens
between that memory of bridesmaids and this one
of owls courting? Those old Greeks had it wrong:

to never have been at all, that would be worst,
to have missed these moments that arrived
unbidden merely because we were here,
never to have woven a lifetime of these
momentary joys into a life—

my dog Finnbarr, asleep on the deck one morning
while a nest-making titmouse plucked hairs from his back,
woke up and turned to the sun, unsurprised,
giving the bird more time to complete its moustache.

Or that moon out the kitchen window, a licorice wafer
fallen from the roll. Until, along its southeastern edge,
a thread of light began, never before in sixty years, maybe
never again, backlit with the silence of October dawn.

The Blue Woods

You sat on the white line
at a bend of Long Pond Road,
if you are who I think you were,
and posed for a snapshot,
daring the lack of traffic
in rolled jeans and saddle shoes,

legs crossed, with a fan of hair
your scarf almost tamed,
back when I hoped *forever*
would pass by high-school osmosis
from my palm into yours.

Whoever you are now, three carts ahead
in the checkout line, I make it
eighteen thousand days
since your face reflected firelight
at Fisher's Beach. Time hasn't softened
everyone in such a generous way.

Your purchases ring up
sensible and spare: children must be
grown and gone, but above
your checkbook and gold ring
that slight puzzlement's still there.

Tell me I'm not so far gone
that if I leaned into your purview
I couldn't bring back the way pine trunks
lay down their shadows, barring the light
with purples across sandy roads,

back when excitement was the sun
oxidizing Nemasket Cola signs
and a deer fleeing us up ahead,
freezing my scalp, was at first
a doberman, every time.

Old Bob Gray coming sudden
around a bend was another bristling moment,

underlined by the locust's buzz,
the town's senior collector of silences,
in high summer his sweat-salted hat
full of blueberries the size of dimes.

Behind rimless glasses, his movie-lifer
face and his bare nod in passing
kept us going toward a skinny-dip pond
with pickerel schooled in its shallows,
plier-mouthed, chained, like hardware
in the flesh,
                    or a heron crossed
so high above us the sun made
transparencies of its wings. Certain
that Bob Gray watched from the trees,
you'd dive through my hands like silk anyway.

Those blue, living, unbroken acres
breathed the underleaf cool of the day
back into the dusk, and whippoorwills,
nightly, were still possible, but
figment or fragment of fifty years ago,
you are gone through the glass doors
into that dark again, memory's
glory hole, where the light in your eye
like a hypnotist's watch
is spinning in my own.

The Potatoes Have a Word to Say

These are the faces we made down there
to entertain each other. We were green,
marble-sized, scabbed over and rutted
when you threw us into the compost
last fall. After nights of rain that swelled
and softened the earth so we wondered
how any of you anywhere ever thought
it was flat, we returned from exile
and you shoveled us under the rototiller
to be rendered impossible. Fiddleheads
down in the marsh arose from their own
torn parchment and mummy cloth,
and we shoved up, thick-stemmed among
the early unfurlings of squash and beans,
and in evenings of broken thrush music
began drawing gold-centered,
lavender starbursts out of ourselves,
in concert with the sleeping trees:
red dwarfs in the maples, constellated
petals of wild apple. We had toughened up
in that rejects' underworld the chickweed
flourished over. Now you have drawn us
into September, volunteers caught out
in our proletarian jackets, but don't
misread us. Whether as slave food
or aphrodisiac, we have always been
in politics, and though never educated
like the artichoke, or fopped-up
like certain squashes, we can be multiplied
by anyone, prepared more ways than bread.
You are tired of living when you're tired of us.

Mushrooms

A rain of acorns woke us
to another summer slept away.
On stumps and treefall
we arose, irruptions
as dark-minded as yours,

or else a punkwood
rigadoon, or lowfalutin'
parliament: old men of
the woods; sad why-men
in a conclave under
medieval hats; sitwells;

satchells and sacheverells.
Look here: this cup and flask,
jellies, an orange peel,
oysters and a strew of lemons
sliced, a chocolate cone,

or else, depending on your view,
a ground like Spotsylvania
after the artillery rolled away,
or a wild haberdashery: cloche
and sombrero, turbans, wimples.

We blush and pale,
like you. Like you we are
mostly water, and live upon
decay. Autumn Coletti,
is that one of us, or the girl
you loved in seventh grade?

If, in our names, you find
a cast, Slippery Jack,
the rogue; Grisette, the little
match girl; the vamp False
Chanterelle; Silky Volvaria,
the racetrack tout,

even the foreign airline Fly
Agaric, too many characters
will break your story down, and we
break down: this brief prime
is our beauty, too soon
we deliquesce upon ourselves—

No rose without manure,
as you might say. Come here
at midnight and a few of us
will glow for you. On Mars
we would have been
the debutantes.

Four Things Charlie Fox Loved

were apples, horses, and giving apples
   to horses, and floating bareback
on a Percheron named Gabe—wide as

a parlor rug and slow as a summer
   Sunday afternoon cloud—up the Stone
Arabia Road, through Illyrium Center,

Limekiln, Hammett, Starkville, some Sundays
   even as far as Bremen Lake before he'd
turn Gabe homeward. Better to check on

a couple of early ripeners than snore
   good daylight away, he'd tell you,
an after-dinner belly like a stone

dropping you through every level of sleep.
   He could see past the Aggie pamphlets,
and by its long, upright stem and yellow flesh

he knew a Sweet June that survived the notice
   of the horticultural boys behind a barn
silvered with abandonment, its loft

a purple martin lodge, the house
   out front a settlement of dust. Fruit yellowish,
under the middle size (politely put), sweet

and rich, though not an ideal keeper—this
   Thacher wrote in 1822, and as an afterthought:
chief apple of the Plymouth colony.

Sweet-June, sweet-sweet-June, Charlie Fox
   could even hear an apple-colored goldfinch
singing in the name, singing from the tree

to tell the name to whoever it was had stood
   three hundred miles, three hundred years
behind him by that bay, admiring the grandsire

of this tree. So Gabe could take his pick, Charlie
    stepped him right up to the branches—the martins
sweeping in and out the barn, blue-green as stars

across the afternoon—and thought, *A country that's
    lost track of its apples is headed off to hell on a handcar,*
then balanced on Gabe's back to fill his pockets.

Apple Muse

Charlie Fox will look up from oatmeal
and coffee at six this morning
and see the only waterthrush all year
bobbing at the seed table out his window,
and that will be my first sign. All night
after yesterday's rain I have turned the wind
out of the northwest toward Charlie's
whereabouts, and seeded it with birds
so this afternoon a house wren
will follow his tomcat home, buzzing
like a joke tied to its tail, my second sign.

A cool night in August like this one
and the flesh of Holland Pippins and Reinettes
begins to surge. I can feel the orchard
shake as though each tree's being shivered
by a bear stocking up for a long sleep.
This morning a line of drizzle will hang
its dismal laundry above Charlie's meadow,
way down where that red buck like an early
leaf-change raises its eight-point rack
out of grass, wet muzzle working.

That's another sign I've sent him,
with the inchling toad he'll stoop for,
crossing the yard. He'll keep his fist closed,
as on a stone, warming it until it nuzzles
his palm, then Charlie will let it leap
for the congregation of morning glories.

He'll be sharpening the cutter bar by some old
corner of Queen Anne's lace and goldenrod
one of these cider-lit afternoons,
and I'll swing the breeze for censer and stop him
cold: apple musk, aroma, tang? Standing there
with his nose going at the air like a beagle's,
he'll have no adequate word for the mystery
that stuns him yearly. It's unfair, I know.

Charlie Fox might have been the Midas
of corn or alfalfa, but it matters what a man
loves, and one day he bit into
a Kittagaskee Wonder and there I was.

Winter Stars

There's nothing more to be said, except,
one of these nights, Orion will throw
a frost-brilliant leg over the dunes again,

and we'll hear the rote of surf once more,
the peninsula beginning to breathe free
of sunblock and outlandish dreams.

By the time that star-man returns
in silence from wading the salt oceans,
every loud talker in the post office,

even those joggers with ears
electronically bunged against birdsong
on Corn Hill Road,
                              will be dragged
back under the weight of ambition
that presses down on cities,

and all these summer supplement
artists will be gone, their reputations
faded like heat ripples at the town line.

Then we'll be the only light keepers
on our square mile of the planet. Delicious
to think of it, and of taking the long way

to Ciro's again for *zuppa, calamari,
scampi,* no need for reservations when
Orion climbs farther away from the bleeping

inane, the blather of honchos inventing
themselves on cell phones. Starlight. Silence.
Our thirty-five years under winter stars together.

Testament

As for me, I'm going to keep shoving these fists
full of sickle asters in your face. Especially
when your car's broken down at roadside
and you're quaking because you don't know
what's waiting for you beyond the asphalt.
When you dread the appearance of ants
in your kitchen, I'm going to describe how
they percolate out of cupboards, that's the word,
then tell you more about apples
than you ever wanted to know: how that core
you tossed from your passing car
sprung a tree no thicker than a surf-casting rod,
which supports this booty that's weighing
my pockets down. Go ahead, walk away, close
your ears and vote with your feet. Nothing
I can tell you will fatten your checking account,
and there's nothing here to lionize. There's only
unpretending life, present and accounted for,
the cerulean warbler's brittle stance a moment
on the railing, intrepid for the run to Ecuador.
Which refutes all slaves of theory and returns them
to their gestures. Remember the morning
that black-tailed godwit from Eurasia probed the mud
between the salt pond and a sandspit the color
of its neck? That was me behind you
whispering how—separate and together, absorbed
and linked into other forms, laid in new knots
of protein, entered without will in xylem
and panicle—we might draw a wondering crowd
like us into another moment like that one.
It wasn't to frighten you, but to speak
of fecundity, as even this inchworm knows,
who lives in my notebook, and sometimes omega,
sometimes parenthesis, steps off the lengths of
these lines, and is strong as the guffaw
I woke myself with one night, for no reason
I could find on either side of sleep.

The Strength of a Named Thing (1999)

Pondycherry

The way some people sing for themselves
on the drive home, I kept repeating
pondycherry out loud, one of those
trivial chunks that pops up,
tangled with the mind's sargassum,

and wondering where I got it, arrived at
a satiny red-brown wood that came
naturally hollowed from the mill, something
a craftsman might use in his furniture,

an elderly wood-turner and caner of chairs
who worked out of a storefront, its floor
lovely to the nostrils and eyes
with sawdust and woodcurl.

He'd be a local repository who still used
honeywicket for flicker, *timberdoodle*
for woodcock. He'd look at
a yard-sale chair, its seat busted
through like a basketball hoop, and say,

"That wood's pondycherry, used to be
a stand of it the far side of Higgins Pond.
A pleasure to work with, but the fruit
would pucker you permanent."

Pondicherry, the dictionary gives me,
a former province of French India.
But why should I choose between denotation
and the mind at play, or reject another
hint from the depths under a word
that I've lived other places, other lives?

Brother Francisco Anthony Eats an Apple

After the first bite watered his thirst,
the bouquet ignited some recall. Was this
second-sight, or memory in the cambium
between the flaking bark and heartwood,
where history sticks,
thin as paper yet immortal?

Brother Francisco Anthony, monk
and pomologist, in an Upham orchard,
the trees reverting to wild root stock,
throwing themselves back out of Suffolk
into happenstance. He claimed
in his *Sylva Sylvarum* of 1520
he could taste dispersals in
that golden apple, a hint
of thatch afire, smoke funneling
to the sky, a channel crossing
in a bowman's sack.

He saw a Norman fletcher
pluck it on the road to St.-Malo, 1065,
then tribal palimpsests, migrations,
horsemen, their blades flashing back
across the dark of Europe into
the wild groves of the Caucasus:
Alma Alta, "Father of Apples," its trees
hung with shapes as various as
the faces of those who journeyed there
to twist fruit from the branches
and sugar their bitter lives.

No cider without seasons,
Brother Francisco wrote, *or child*
without a ripeness, no beauty
without flaw, as all rugmakers know
who botch one knot in homage
to the day a lie was told
that brought change to the leaves
and drew down snow. He saw

that apple fallen from a suddenly
fatal hand. The print of perfect teeth
skewed and began to brown
in its flesh, a white mouth whispering
rot among the roots. *Their choice
was immortality,* he said, *or never
to have tasted this fruit.*

Listening to the Garden

Look at it this way: under the brass fanfare
of their blossoms, all those zucchinis
are really incipient oompahs.
And the pea-vine tremolos? Middle C
rubbed out of a rhubarb stalk?

Now you're beginning to hear it: that line
of radishes ostinato, bean paradiddles,
a beefsteak tomato redballing its cadenza.

Aren't the parts of these vegetables—the phloem,
the calyx and carina—names of woodwinds
you'd love to hear, in counterpoint
with the garden's valves and bells?

Remember that morning you drove
into the main street of a town—Colorado Springs,
was it?—on no holiday you could name?

Nevertheless, the high school band was passing,
majorettes in their short, flippant skirts
frilled like the inner linings of lettuce,
and shakos, corn-tassel plumed, remember,

and the frogging on jackets—cucumber vines
scrolled on themselves. The whole garden's
flash and patootle was moving off
toward a snowed-upon peak
down at the end of that street.

The Soul Is Not Colorless

Nine A.M. growl of withdrawing bolts,
and the branch manager leans into
double-thick folding doors and turns,
footsore, without even a glance
at the morning, toward the bank's
glass façade, and as if it was waiting
for him in the low maintenance
evergreen by the door, a mourning cloak
butterfly leaps up, brown as
the paneling in a room
squared to regulations, but with
marginal yellow bands below
a blue spotty fringe, sunlight
and sky forced to the edges,
the view from a small window.
For the soul is never colorless:
it can move through its time as a great
purple hairstreak over a meadow,
go flopping and lurching, a checkerspot
through milkweed, be a yellow
dogface composing itself on dogbane,
or beat at a man's blue suit,
a dream of flight evicted and battling
to get back under his skin.

Toad

Trencherman of the moist places,
I never find you at home in your cracked
flowerpot under the day lilies,
but drinking through your skin, asleep
or unperturbed by my shoe in a wet furrow.
To live you have to bury yourself
alive sometimes, risking a tine when
I fork the compost and the earth
caves there and quakes. Undercover cop
of the garden, you are serious
as a samurai, and shoot from the lip,
cleaning up on ten thousand pests
in a good season. Have a couple of
spittlebugs, chase them down
with a red-banded leaf-hopper or two,
but lay off those geishas the ladybugs,
who have work of their own to do.
Were you dropped here, a meteorite
of green-crusted ore? Nights
when the moon's your color, I imagine
Japan, and a farmer who throws
the first cup from the bottle
into his fields as a welcome to you.

Pelican

That look of a singular relic
blown out of the annals
of evolution, such mock-seriousness
turned loose on this world
they might have dubbed me
"Pelican" as early as high school,

not merely for my addiction
to wharves and my vertigo
out of sight of tidal habitats,
but for broad-flippered feet
that still make me
hard to follow on dancefloors,

and for the way, late at night,
trying to make it home
in my black Filene's Basement
clerical trenchcoat (but lined in
cardinal red!), I'd flap
a few strokes, then sail and
flap a few more, the whole getup
assembled to suggest
a saving naïveté.

Then there's my approach to
necessity, not the direct sharp
plunge of a gannet, all torque
to an economical vanish, but
the splash of some bulk
a deckhand rolls over the side
as soon as land
has cleared the horizon.

If they stuck around
after that splatter, they'd have
seen it was all in knowing
the exact angle for entry,
sheer technique so I come up
sitting every time, making

those swallowing movements
that assure I will never
go hungry, operating on
too many levels at once,
the usual crowd of laughing gulls
hanging around for crumbs.

Captain Teabag and the Wellfleet Witches

Red-gold her hair the one night,
a crow's gloss the next, and the tall
or short of her apparently as
she chooses, Silkpocket's the one
who taught me her way of dreaming
where the oysters gather, nights
she'd leave me to my bed alone.
Put it in my head, you might say,
so if I sailed to the dream place
next day I'd drag up such a weight
as would draw the portside
like a lip to the waves. Taught me
a rhyme for summoning breezes
from nowhere even in blue calms,
another for settling tall seas.
Two feats I'd not perform for even
a crowd of one, as per her warning.
Or only once I did, and here's that story:
Off Jeremy one noon it kicked up
some ferocious. My sheets bellied
and it blew a hat-swiper
so the boy hunched to the tiller
two-handed while I crept along
the freeboard like an ape escaping
down a clothesline on all fours,
then crouched in the bow yelling
Silkpocket's verses at the teeth of it,
wind spitting them back drenched,
salting them line by line and driving
every word into my throat and eyes
until I heard because I couldn't see
the canvas crack and flap to
a standstill. Those airs left
whistling in a ball across the headland
and the sun stood out again,
dulling the depths while I dreaded
how I'd catch it from her that night,
for the boy was studying me like

he'd caught me weighting oyster sacks
with stones. Silkpocket taught me . . .
many things. And sure enough, she got
her hooks in me that night out by the Gut,
crooning *Come to me, my palomino.*
Off we went, down the Neck road
at a gallop. You see how my knees
are skunned up yet, for it took us
a few rods before she got me
in the air, my ears between her
cunning thumbs and forefingers
the way you'd turn a key in a lock.
We cleared Shirttail Point
and *Haul those elbows in!* she screeched,
and veered me starboard of that
windmill whicketing around
next the saltworks, then shot us out
up Duck Creek and twice around
the Congregational steeple,
Silkpocket digging those red shoes
in my slats and pushing me at speeds
I lack the sheer for, so by then
I'm chafed and rasped all over.
"We'll have a little drinkie," she says
close to my ear, that mean kind
of babytalk she has, and dips us
in this fog that's dripping over
the Herring River. About that time
I know I'm going to come to alone
and feeling like six sacks of owl pellets
freshmade. Escape her? Sure.
I got as far as Loagy Bay once,
then up come this cloud over the boat
kept changing colors like some gypsy stone
only all its moods was bad? Each way
I tacked it stuck. Calm, flat and blue
was everywhere but where I was.
Then three crows hung up there yacking

under it and the bay commenced to flap
and boil and pitch around, black and oily
as they were. Soon after twenty more
showed up from nowheres, batting around
in the sheets, perched on the gunnels,
tiller, anywhere in the way and everywhere
at once. My gear was a holy tangle
and me with a gaff and as much sense
as a bear in a bee storm slashing around.
All the witches of Wellfleet were there—
Old Margery Gigg the icehouse lady
rode my yawing tiller like a laughing
weathercock. I swung at one and it was
Hamm the postman, I'd know the wrecked
picket-fence of his teeth anywhere,
though up to then I only suspected
he snuck the village's letters home
for something to read, that lonely place
he lives, sunk to the sills in weeds.
Spanish Mariah from out Bound Brook way,
Annie down the oyster shacks,
they were there, and several beansupper
Christians including that moist-handed
Banker Leverett in his sister's bonnet,
gone all to nose and snapping like
a hairless raccoon. Some others
Silkpocket must of sent out of town for,
or signed up in the graveyard. No words I have
could tell you what sobfellows and nobaths
were there, what skroaks and wowsy-eyed
giglets, drabboons, a loptongue or two,
craven-haired skewbabes and bouncies,
pisscutters, bloats, fluffchicks,
retching simps, flarks, bigbighairs
and reeking bone-rigged doglets,
barffleas. Does that add up to
more than twenty? Well I was counting
poorly at the time, and snaggling

about with them in my gear whilst they were
subdividing, tripling, swapping off
one another's best parts all the time
we were going down. Next I know
Silkpocket's got me by the topmost hairs
and hauling me out. "Good grip on you,"
I says, and she says back, "My love
is on the dear one." That being me,
I guess, so how could I escape her
after that? Looks like I'm never
going to know if I'll come to in my bed
or curled up on Holbrook Avenue
one sunrise to the next.

A Warning to the Comet Hyakutake about the Olafsen Brothers

At first you were only a smear
a bird could leave on the new
bathroom skylight, then a barely moving
midnight bonus for all we overpaid

those two other chunks of solar
system debris and alleged
carpenters, the Olafsen brothers,
Skew-hammer and Skimpwood.

But nine point three million miles
straight up, they say, and forty-five
times faster than a speeding bullet,

it could only be you where the stars
we had this glass installed for
plod through their routes.

From another fragile body like yours,
from the heart of my own emissions
and gasses, I swear I feel privileged,
not minuscule, under your presence,

fearing more that we humans may be
alone in the cosmos with a couple of
other hard crusts on icy nuclei.

Safe journey then. If you see a pickup
held together with duct tape, driven
by a man with a dog, or his brother
as dog substitute, by these signs

you will know those Olafsen brothers,
who do all their thinking at the corners
of their eyes, and could therefore
conceivably reach you and make trouble.

My Frost Dream

Farm boys on a hillside in New Hampshire,
shirtsleeves rolled past their elbows,
waiting for a train to pull into a station
down below—Franconia, maybe, or Potter Place—
and take them off to war. A blonde girl stands
by one of them: to get her blue-flowered
'40s housedress and wild beauty on the page,
Frost the botanist compares her
to a roadside weed, the Venus's Looking glass.
She speaks of merging her father's farm
with her soldier boy's, the dynasty they'll start
after the war. Behind her words Frost's hinting
that the boy won't be coming home, though all
he'll say outright is, "Two farms are more
than twice the work." This poem's more 20th
century than anything of his yet in print,
I tell him, studying the typescript, and since
this is my dream, not Lawrance Thompson's,
he takes the compliment agreeably, and asks
my name. Where are we, Bread Loaf? Cambridge?
We're standing on a sofa making smalltalk,
our heads way above the party racket. When
X the poet comes by, a voice out of the air
says, "Prepare to be cut dead," and Frost
says, "X, meet Brendan Galvin . . ."

Wheelbarrow

Though I have come to it late,
something in the balance
and trundle of it
full of earth appeals to
something in my bones
about bearing up,

unreasonably evokes my
father's face that morning
clouds massed over him
and wind panicked
the white-capped mile
of blackening pond he rowed
two sons across, all three of us
soaked in wave-smash
off the bow. It feels

good to me, this tipcart
like the one my grandfather
wheeled bricks and mortar
up the Irish gangplanks in,
helping Boston to rise
beyond his reach,
then pushing out along

the river where
the triple-deckers began,
bearing up when Mary Barr
lifted her skirts and
stepped in, then one by one,
little Mimi, Billy, Kath,
John, Lena, and Jimmy, lifetimes
of bearing up, so now

I'm rolling back along
that route edged with eelgrass,
going east toward origins,
above me a flight of black-crowned
night herons limping home

like workers off a graveyard
shift, then in and out of stained-glass
baptistries, vow-makings,
the West End streets of old men
singing *Baruch, Baruch, Adonai*
as they walk, palms outward,
releasing their joy to the air.

Wheelbarrow, fit vehicle for
that cartoon ape-slouch
the Know Nothings welcomed
greenhorns with, slurring it
"Paddy's rowboat," "the Irish
dowsing-rod" I bought to move
loam and firewood, but bowed
to it feeling bloodlines flow

until I'm shadowed by the El's
steel lattice past Brink's garage
and the molasses tanks,
looking for Half Moon Alley,
Hungry Hill, Kerry Village where
the strong-nosed, ruddy arrivals
spoke a revenant poetry over
their tea and bread, and handcarts
rumbled their household burdens
door to door, looking for home.

At Ellen Doyle's Brook

Since there's no childhood
without a witch, the children had
some mockery they chanted
in your brogue when they danced
up the dust around your cottage.

Counterpoint to Baileyville's
laundry ghosting on your lines,
was it worse than the silences
their elders used, or is all that
a question of temperament?

As soon pin you down now as capture
your washwater in this stream
they gave your name. You were
different, elusive as your brook's
obscure beginnings and ends,

and sentenced between silences,
you starched their tatted
handkerchiefs you thought were
doilies, amusing to some
even now their song's escaped them.

This water you made yours
a bucket at a time
beats any stone memorial, as the wrecked
millrace attests, and anyone who reads
your moods in leaf-defended

pools—where something gray
whispers itself up to the risk
of one quick sip, or a fleeting yellow
jumps in, spontaneous as a laugh,
and shaking, springs off through the trees—

must see this water underwritten
by hill snows, digesting ice, muscling up
with rain to wash the road out
and beat back underground any prize rose
a lady bequeaths her name.

Web Sights

Some look geodesic, while others are gothic
on seedheads dried and ready for dispersal.
Still others are plumblines dropped from pines,
and over there's a bombsight, here's the Big Top
just before the canvas goes up, trampolines
in the grass, armatures of fog, even something
that recalls a little item Sophia Loren wore
for a devastating moment. If you were
an arachnophobe you wouldn't get out of bed
this morning, and if I were Charles Burchfield
I'd stand for eternity at this place on
Corn Hill Road where sickle asters toss
their purple in a potpourri with goldenrod
and rosehips, backed by marshgrass
gilding away from green. But all these
components lying around, as though someone
gave up on assembling their silver idea of a world,
not sunlight's, and not necessarily this world,
and chucked the parts into the weeds last night.

The Vegetable

1.

Two weeks to Halloween and this thing
is still mottled in greens. Maybe it's
the Sasquatch of squashes, or something
new to display at the state fair, but it's nothing
we planted, nothing we've ever seen
in a catalog. As though one summer night
a rogue seed gathered its strength
out there, and leapt across several stages
of evolution, or else the moonlight
brought a couple of veggies together,
and here we have the zupkin. The plant
that pushed it out has collapsed, and that thing
seems to be drawing it through the umbilicus
to its bosom. What's next? A rococo crust,
a rat in livery, a wild ride to
the Agricultural Extension? It's clear
there isn't going to be any
"You taste it first." "No, you."

2.

And now, as though a zupkin did
my spirit steal, the word if not the thing
has wormed its way for two months
up my brain stem to the core. Somewhere
behind the *os frontalis* it's tickling like
a grade school song at memory and meaning:
Zupkin, Zupkin I've been thinking.
Or else he was that aide of Trotsky's,
forehead pale in the camera flash, glasses
rimless, dark suit and mustache
one with the background. Zupkin,
looking like some bloodless prof
condemned to be forever tenureless,
until his name becomes generic,
as in, *It's Zupkinsville for him.*
And for this vegetable as well, its pith
contracted, cortex olive drab and rubbery,
tossed in among the peels and rinds of things
that had names once, and may again.

Charlie Fox

Tell me again how he led the Percherons
Mike and Gabe out of his barn
when you were a little girl, and stood
between them so you feared for him

because they had the chests of archangels
and he was built as if by someone who'd studied
a problem and made him to solve it.

Do they anymore come that wiry? I would
put the question his way, who plowed
with his feet on the ground, no Allis-Chalmers
or John Deere foolery, and that afternoon

told your father, *Promise or go home.*
If I sell you this farm you must care for
Gabe and Mike until their time.

Tell me how he used his after-years tracking down
old apple trees, restoring the taste buds
with Stone Arabia Pearmains, Ephrata Russets,
Three Pond Roseblooms,

naming them where he found them, wedding
their scions to root stock, his Ford pickup
crow-black and crow-far against golden walls

of cornstalk climbing all the way to a sky
above Canada, *Because apples are partial*
to starlight and the cold, or they'll taste like
you're chewing on your coat sleeve.

Though it never could happen, he might have been
speaking of himself: *It's all in the lumps and skews.*
Heft and looks are nothing.

Best apple I ever ate was square and yellow,
but blushing. Tell me how he said, *When you prune,*
cut back till you could toss a cow through the tree
and never harm a twig, and I'll tell you the name
of the man they should have buried at Avalon.

Walter Anderson Sleeping on the Levee

In New Orleans to research Hurricane Betsy,
the one he'd ridden out tied to a tree trunk
on Horn Island, he rolled up for the night
on the levee by Audubon Park, letting
the Mississippi talk him to sleep.
Surrounded again, as on the island,
toward morning he felt the serious eyes,
and waited on the moment they'd show themselves.
He saw for the one and only time
the carcasson, then the smaragdine
and gallowglass, but were these the names
of birds, or the names of birds
he wished there were? If a bird is a hole
in heaven through which a man may pass,
then what in the hell were all these anxious
steppers? No pouldeau or pelican, nothing
he'd ever sketched or done in watercolors,
no redwing or boat-tailed grackle
that waited for raisins and cold rice
he'd fling them from last night's supper.
The hurricane, he figured, had lifted
these strangers out of the park's aviary.
Could they sense that he'd talked with
the morning star, or escaped from hospitals
because authority amused him? He was
necessary again: on the levee these birds
would starve or be brought down by
an air rifle or household beast. Casting
breadcrumbs over his shoulder, he led them
back into the park, wrestling their names
from himself, pied piper of the stonechuck
and pripet, the fireneck, peabill,
mer-hen, the garget, the stant.

Sky and Island Light (1997)

Skylights

Every October, after a day when something
exotic has landed at the feeder
and waits gasping there as on a prow
far out at sea, a myrtle or Canada warbler
just too wing-beaten to go on,
I wake late to a good dinner
building its cloud above my heart,
and look up where stars in the skylight
on that night alone have a connect-the-dots
logic, a plan I might follow that's pressing
like a template in my head. Then I envision
the great streaming freeways of the birds,
those swerves and swoopings in every
color of feather, three miles up, blurred
Crayola streaks a hemisphere long, and
Surinam, French Guiana, Venezuela
loom in a summer down there
like the eminence of a new green heart.
I play around with gravity and magnetic
lines of force trined with the pull of the moon,
but panic hearing the surf of a different
coast in each ear, and drop to name
real hills instead: Tom's and Cathedral
enfolding an arm of river between
bay and ocean; Round and Corn, between
the freshwater lens my pump taps into
and those stars. Husband, father to sleepers,
doorman to dogs, I can't convert pasta
to vector energy anyway. I might say
something I ate causes this,
and tip an invisible nightcap
to the birds, who know where they're going
and how to get there.

Nimblejacks

Remember Hot Spats and the Kaiser,
who illustrated the beautiful
moving-while-standing-still word
nimblejack, a word worthy of
a class of sailboats, like sneakbox,
or sharpie? I'm talking soupbeards
and rent-laggards like Boofer,
who checked out the coinbox on every
payphone in town. I'm talking
skewfooted Dr. Highpockets, who'd share
the sandwich in his carrot bag with anyone.
When was the last time Pungie
yawped at you across the street to say
how well that new puddle was doing
on the wrong side of the dike?
How about Tick, and the Man of Steel,
walk-ons from normality's hinterland,
part of the 9 percent who never have an opinion?
They were the canaries in our mineshaft,
our early warning systems, and never
disappeared into the shops all day,
but stayed on the sidewalks to hinder
the broom of the future simply by being there.
Not one ever asked, "Are you affiliated
with any academic institution?"
or propped Einstein's essays
strategically in a window of the Land Rover,
but remember how they used to line us up
in their sights on Main Street,
leaning left and right to keep us level?

One for the Life List

Not a yellowthroat,
not a yellow warbler, but a
yellow-throated warbler—
it has happened again: the sky
moving out of the west
and before the clouds
migrants come scudding,
so many so fast that the pines
are mobile with blue backs
and bay breasts switching places,
undertail coverts flicking
yellow, white, twitching among
branches, impossible to locate
fast enough, but as though
at the end of summer
an East European primitivist
had painted a Christmas tree
whimsical with birds.
A yellow-throated warbler, one
for the life list, though
I promised myself again
I'd swear off this year.
Instead I've come back
for just one more, a failed
teetotaler of birds,
and better this stupefaction at
a lemon-bibbed ounce of
feathers than the shoddy
illusion of the aloneness
of things, wherein the sky
pours down oceanic emptiness
and the life of a grove migrates
across the road to the gas pumps:
even the common foreground
chickadee and background crow
give dimension to our days,
and not to salute such
charity of song

though it be plain as
thumbsqueaks on clear windowpanes,
not to say their names,
and the shadow of death passes
across our tongues.

Rained Out

That wide bay rippled with just
breeze enough, our tacking a mere tilted
luff of sails, and we circled
dolphins all afternoon, two in tandem,
or they circled us, always gone
just so long we'd seance-rap
the hull, and give up, then
five feet off the port side, fin-wheeling
or blowing in our wake, they'd show,
always in the least, last over-the-shoulder
place, eluding all suggestions
of a watery corral, tail-dancing
a half-mile off, sea hams bringing
again and again the gift
of their curiosity, humoring our own
under slow clouds piled white toward
the sun and deepening blue
where they faced oncoming evening,
with clusters of flight here and there,
first August signs of pre-flocks
forming up, and that one broad
underbelly of cloud over
Great Island and the Gut, gray, hairy,
taking its time, looking like something
you might find on the floor beneath
a long-standing frigidaire, then,
over us, letting go not rain
exactly, but fat, single,
ringing drops you could walk between
if you could walk on water,
each with its own pitch, fingerbells
on a delicate Asian hand,
gracenotes on the tide, lasting only
the moment such things can, passing on
toward headlands and the world
of evening light falling into
the harbor's stand of masts,
and the dolphins: gone.

A Cold Bell Ringing in the East

It woke me to this full moon
just pulling away
from the skylight's pine,
and fire in the stove's window
faint as two owls courting
somewhere in these empty woods.
Was it the cold I let in
when I let the dog out
that reduced everything to images,
stripping the rags off ego
and abstraction, shivering
the shadows of the pines?
In this light all our attempts
at this or that mean nothing,
we live by understanding less
than there is in the nose
of this dog construing the air.
That pine is no inn,
the moon's no Chinese courtesan
departing from it a thousand
years ago, and I am not Li Po.
There are those who envy that stone
its decoder-ring luminosity, and those
who would sell the tree.
What joy in having been at all,
in feeding the fire and knowing
that everything isn't about us.
Who can witness these moments
and edges otherwise, except someone
outside them, without
the camouflage of a horned lark,
and praise the virtues of scrub pines
with guardian shapes of sky
among them on these hills?
Only someone not woven into
that fabric, with no protective

coloring, who sees where a deer
is first air, then color of dusk
in scrub, then dusk itself,
with its air of invisible mending.

Pococurante

Word for the ringsnake
I found in a burl
just under the woodpile tarp,
folded like a black mat of
witches' butter fungus,
trying to shunt itself
its own failing heat, asleep,
so I worked around it,
splitting the pile and facing
the open sides up elsewhere
until, a foot long, longer,
snake poured itself through
itself, down one layer, showing
a yellow collar, and curled
again between two rounds,
buried its head, pococurante,
caring little, like a
stove-settled dog, and as its
tenements disappeared
with the afternoon, spilled
down oak, layer by layer, all
the way to damp earth,
where, discombobulous, it rolled
and stiffened, yellow belly
up, one of those gimp
lanyards woven in childhood,
and I made it a teepee of
bark sleeves to withdraw
from October in, and went away.

For a Daughter Gone Away

Today there've been moments
the earth falters and almost
goes off in those trails of smoke
that resolve to flocks so far
and small they elude my naming.
Walking the old Boston & Maine
roadbed, September, I understand
why it takes fourteen
cormorants to hold the bay's
rocks down. Have I told you
anything you ought to know?
In time you'll come to learn
that all clichés are true, that
a son's a son till he marries,
and a daughter's a daughter
all her life, but today
I want to begin Latin I with you
again, or the multiplication
tables. For that first phrase of
unwavering soprano that came
once from your room, I'd suffer
a year of heavy metal. Let all
who believe they're ready for
today call this sentimentality,
but I want the indelible
print of a small hand
on the knees of my chinos again,
now that my head's full of
these cinders and clinkers
that refused fire's refinements.
I wish I could split myself
to deepen and hold on as
these crossties have, and admit
goatsbeard and chicory,
bluecurls and blazing star,

these weeds of your never quite
coming back. I wish I could stop
whatever's driving those flocks
and drove the B & M freights into air.

The Portuguese Uncle

There was a grove next door
where we scuffed pine needles
to floor plans for other houses
with no wars over groceries, no
maiden aunts penumbral
with desertion, and no grownups
whose remarks to us
nearly disguised their alternate
meanings. Otherwise, we sat
failing on the kitchen steps,
or smoked a hardball through
the morning glories
until Uncle Manny herded us
to his beetle-backed Studebaker
and we drove into his country,
its high smell of fish
snapping us out of it. In rooms
above the wharves talk exploded
in both languages, the one for
cursing hard paymasters
in front of children, the other
for saying the cod went north
and weren't coming back, things
illustrated by hands scored
with the drag of halibut
on droplines. We nursed orange
or grape drinks at enameled
tables, the men sun-browned in
red shirts, with matadors'
smooth hair and noses you tried
not to look at, hands folded
for bottomless silences, in which
to count gulls kiting past
the windows. Once our uncle
yelled, "Popeye!" and there he was,
the anchor cap, the squint,
his corncob in that loaf of chin—

at the door of the plant where
women ripped out orange spawn
and dropped it to the floor,
where trawlers sidling to the wharf
shook the world's tin roof
and spiles and at the scales
lumpers and crews might erupt
out of nothing over prices, where
noon-shriek drove those women
arching in their clothes
one by one to the rainbowed water
we'd dare to enter ourselves, sometime,
we said later, alone, and splash
and kick and swim among them
when they came up, lipstick redder,
hair pasted black, wet
to their true shapes.

Anchorites

1. *On the Saints' Road*

Pilgrim again, over those ancient
cattle tracks pressed into service
as national highways, wherever
the Guide to Ireland inflated
a vestige of half-buried stones
to a saint's tale, or injected
the least trickle with miracles,
I picked my way through
a glossary of belief: Reask,
Kilmalkedar, Labbamolaga. While the wind
piled rain on the stones, my spirit
stumbled and crashed about in its
puffin mask like someone at a party
coming unglued, sick of benign
explanations for everything
under the sun. I wanted beyond craving
some wonder and mystery
mortared with crushed shells, horsehair,
milk, and feculence, some blunt
and basic anchorite
with the cold-boned authority
eras of Atlantic weather convey
to step round-eyed
from his stone and beat hell
and humanism out of me,
screaming, "This is the way!"
It never happens, of course. But
once, home a week, passing
the John Hancock Tower, my unforgetting
cochlea released across evening fields
a West Country cuckoo call, an answer
of sorts, and I crouched
to the sidewalk, expecting a hail of glass.

2. *Reply to a Saint Patrick's Day Card*

Shamrocks he demonstrated the Trinity
through, they ate. Robed and barbered,
touched with the airbrush, he looks
incapable of stepping ashore somewhere
far down the Rhine and busting up
the local idols with an oar,
or sailing to Iceland's penitential
freeze for the crime of knocking
another bishop down
when a small theological point
turned physical. But in all
the looks and acts of those anchorites,
as in their armpits, there was
more than a touch of the goat:
they could blister cheeks with a curse
or go years without a word,
fearing nothing but the day the sky
might fall on them, and with all
the goat-minded insouciance of art,
carved the name of their savior
in fish-shape on obstructions
to ocean where no one
would want to live but them,
and there prayed so hard
that body-light splayed through
unmortared walls. Given
a minute, they ask too much
of us. Therefore no holidays for them.

Under My Stornoway Hat

Thinking along its designs
that look like the mingled sea routes
of wandering Picts, Celts,
and Norsemen, mumbling the names
of their ports, I see how Scalloway
might render to scallawag,

how all my life, hanging around
harbors, three sheets to the wind
on their air of departures alone—
roadstead, outward bound,
hull down for anywhere, a lingo
that lifts my nape hairs—

I might have become a seaport's
drunk if poems hadn't
grabbed me by the throat.
If I say Caledonian-MacBrayne ,
my pulse rate drops and I'm ready
to sail on just my name

for Stromness or Lerwick or Ullapool,
anywhere oystercatchers and lapwings
stand in for lowly pigeons,
places precipitated onto the sea-line
because they're too blue
for the sky, lumps of holy island
blue as the wool of this hat,
that now and again disappear

and return with more curlews
in a single field than I've counted
in a lifetime. Here in this livingroom,
in this magical blue hat, I see
how Stornoway commends itself
to stowaways, and this sheep-smelling
wool recalls the Soay ram
who told me, side-of-his-mouth
near Scrabster, Keep moving.

Saints in their Ox-Hide Boat (1992)

*F*rom Irish monasticism came the idea of "white martyrdom," of giving up all that one loves by leaving one's religious brethren, kin, and homeland for a solitude in a foreign country or on an island, the better to contemplate God without distractions. If such a pilgrimage was by sea, it was sometimes called a "blue martyrdom," and the most famous of the blue martyrs was the man known now as St. Brendan the Navigator. Born around 484 near Tralee, County Kerry, Brendan established monastic foundations in Scotland, Wales, Brittany, and quite probably the Faroe Islands, as well as Ireland, and his influence spread about the European continent and as far north as the Gulf of Finland. Up to the sixteenth century, he occupied the place in Irish hagiography now reserved for St. Patrick.

We know of Brendan's exploits primarily through the Latin *Voyage of St. Brendan,* written in Ireland perhaps as early as 800, and from various *Lives* and versions of his adventures popular all over Europe throughout the Middle Ages. A reference to his confrontation with a whale appears on the 1513 map of an Ottoman sea captain, and some maps of the Atlantic speculated on the location of a "St. Brendan's Isle" well into the eighteenth century.

How far, in reality, did Brendan sail? We know that Irish monks had lived in the islands off Iceland's coast prior to the Norse arrival there, hence the Vestmannaeyjar (West Men's or Irishmen's) Islands, with their remnant bells and croziers in the Irish manner. Much has been made of the idea that the Promised Land that Brendan's sea-drift monks visited in the *Voyage* was actually somewhere in the New World. In 1976–1977, Tim Severin and his crew, in a vessel approximating those used by the monks—a large ocean-going curragh of tanned ox hides covering a frame of oak and ash, the hull soaked in and regularly replenished with sheep grease for waterproofing—sailed from Ireland along a stepping-stone route, going north to the Hebrides, Faroes, and Iceland, then south under Greenland to the coast of Newfoundland. Severin's feat and subsequent book, *The Brendan Voyage* (1978), not only proved such a journey possible but verified logically some of what appears to be a fictitious, sometimes miraculous sequence of events and encounters in the original Latin *Voyage of St. Brendan*.

While *Saints in Their Ox-Hide Boat* draws on some of the broad details of both the Severin adventure and the anonymous Latin *Voyage*, the characters of Brendan and his monks are my inventions, as are most of the incidents in the poem. One must keep constantly in mind that these men were both religious contemplatives and hardy sailors in a time when no clear distinction between early Christian and late pagan can be drawn, and when monks were sometimes called upon to war for their secular lords.

Likewise, we should not think of them as conforming to a central religious authority. From the time of Christianity's arrival on Irish soil until well after the Synod of Whitby (664) attempted to enforce Roman observances, the faith there was largely supported and spread by monastic houses that sprang up throughout the country. Each was autonomous under the rule of a charismatic abbot, and evolved a liturgy of its own. The combination of spiritual rule and human exemplar was attractive to the Irish, and the monastic foundations were magnets for numerous recruits. Despite an abbot's wish to maintain a small community, his own holiness often drew many to him. We know very little about the foundations' rituals and prayers; that they were not those prescribed by Rome may be evidenced by the fact that even English Jesuits, entering Ireland after Queen Elizabeth's reign, could not recognize some of the ceremonies of Gaelic-speaking believers. To some degree, Rome and her Irish bishops were looked upon as meddlesome, and in Ireland ecclesiastical power was usually held by the local abbot rather than the resident bishop.

B.G.

Without fail these three things
will assure an unlucky sailing:
turning the boat sunward through
three right-hand circles
and standing out of harbor
before the Beltane fires are dead
on spring hillsides; turning your face
toward the waves without prayers
and a fast, for that sea is
no Christian, or brother to any man,
but at best's an uneasy accomplice
who lays no gift of salmon on
anyone's threshold; and taking aboard
a crewman with an edge to his tongue
like a cat's. A boat wants
men who are nimble of mind
and hop spry to orders, no debtors,
fumblers, braggarts, bishops, or loons
to tempt the waters, but a few
with sense, long on muscle and oak,
and better a sharp novice than
two experienced bleaters
whose work is all in their mouths.

My boy, I lay these doings out for you
because I know you were raised
among fields and hills and never
beat your way north beyond the Sheep Islands
or south around Ireland to Wales and Brittany,
and ask that you copy all I tell you
without amendment, whether you consider it
fantastical, or not fantastical enough,
a white head's inventions, who, though
yet sound in body, gapes in his mind
and toothless mouth.

First day of the week, and best
for a journey, before any lark

shook awake to welcome the light,
I followed the stream's waver and spill
among harebells and green thrift,
those little red huts of the blossoming
fuchsia, and avens and sorrel,
down the mountain. All the way
through wet heather, I warmed
into the walk, working my neck
and shoulders to unknot them from a night
on my stone pillow, swinging
my leather satchel past sheep-stare
and sheep-stare, the identical
dumb questions from black faces,
and dropped down out of a cowl of
mist to where the sea was working away
at its niche in the rock, still
and forever honing its discontent,
for all its time in the world.
Our boat waited, ready with water
and mass wine in goatskins, sacked
onions and flat oat loaves, hazelnuts,
dried fish, parsnips, lave, dulse,
and blue sea holly against
the swollen-gum sickness, and a flask
of holy water tucked beneath
the ox skull on her prow.

Singing through the mist came Owen,
a white lucky stone on his neck thong.
No matter how long and well they have
paid with the small of their backs
at an oar, God-burnt and sunburnt,
these old monks are brief sleepers,
and Owen I picked over quicker men
for his wind- and water-reading eye.
It was he that taught me to determine
north by grabbing a louse off myself
and watching how its head
always returns to that direction.
Now Martin—the warrior who came

gore-sick to our abbey and asked
to be taken in, and who no man discovered
in drink from that day—new fish spears
in hand, and limber to risk an arm
at stepping the mast or changing sail.

— Last night, Abbot, he said,
I dreamed a flock of sheep on Eagle Mountain,
wide as a lap of snow across its slope.

A good sign, I nodded, easeless as always
before faring out, and because
I knew what was coming next.

— Ah, but were they climbing the mountain
or coming down? asked Owen.

— What matter is that? I said.

— Well, you see, Brendan, if those sheep
were moving toward higher pasture,
it would mean well for our journey.
But if Martin dreamed them driving
down the hillside, as though
the herdsman's dog was in it . . .

I raised my hand, and would hear no more,
for next he'd be interpreting our sneezes.
Now the shipwright Diarmuid and young
Conor approached with their gear
in satchels, and Conor an otter's pelt
about his waist, for luck. Two
outward-looking men, high-hearted,
each with his ray of sense, sturdy of
mind to endure those times at sea
when all the voices of the past
come out of memory and lurk, laughing
or crying, telling whatever it is
they tell from a blue-black squall
bruising the sky above the mast.

Frisky as goats these two were,
like all young men without women,
like yourself perhaps, though I've
seen no evidence of it. But you too
may be ready on the day when
you have to stand in the gap. Last was
bald Cernan, the smith, a silent man
and intent, as though to tip the cauldron
of his thoughts might spill it all.
Maker of fishhooks, tooth-giver to saws,
tooth-taker from the screeching mouths
of monks, bonesetter, canny with fish oils
at easing strained limbs and quelling
headaches. For all his power above
iron and fire, one faint lift of the head
was his greeting all around.

— Father, Diarmuid said, as I came out
the clochan door a cock crowed.

My head began its swimming. Then Conor,
stitcher of boatskins:

— When I rose from my oatcakes, my stool
heeled over as though some unseen hand
were in the situation.

As always, the old persuasion here,
and best stepped lightly around, if ever
we were to get on the water.

— No good will come of our dipping a single oar
this day, announced Owen. A nod went round
the knot of men, and since that looked to be
the drift of it, we would try again tomorrow,
for whoever would go looking for sanctum
over seas had best begin on a firm right foot.

And why turn my back on Ireland again
to tempt that ocean with the souls of these
five monks? To cancel with music

a curragh makes on the waves
the hammering and dust of our community,
overrun by recruits slack-jawed with admiration
and always in the way—so many you'd think
nobody ever died—and the endless talk
that runs around in circles like those
pocked in stone by the first people?
Or to break from that abbey's yoke
out across limits to where sand, sea,
rock, and sky scrub acedia from the mind,
and point a new way to God, who is a fire
that shapes Himself different on whatever
path He's approached by, yet stays the same?
Or to tangle my spirit in nets of pride?
Nights on the mountain, I churned these questions
without arriving at a solid answer.

Next morning Martin waited by the curragh,
up to his knees in the creek, imploring
help for our journey, his arms spread like
our Master's on His Cross. Conor and Owen
clattered over the stones, and soon
all six were gathered.

— Into the boat, I ordered.

Good fortune, Diarmuid replied, as if to
make restitution for yesterday. Already
I have seen a raven hopping about
my path, white feathers in his wings.

— But a little bright-headed wren
called to me on the way, Conor said.

— Now here is a case where the one may
cancel the other, Owen began. But from
what direction did the little one call?
For if it called from the north, then
a visit from in-laws may be expected.

— He has no in-laws, he's a celibate monk!
I shouted. Ah, the little bird-faced man.

I thought to give him a thump
to shut him up.

— Then it were best we sail toward the south,
Owen replied.

— We are sailing north, I said, fearing
my red beard and tonsure of those days
would crackle and burn off like straw on fire,
leaving me bare skulled as Cernan, who now,
discomfited, was staring from us at the creek.

— But if that wren called from the west,
Owen went on, then perhaps we should not
sail at all, since there are only fields
and mountains to the east. And death tidings
are on us if it called from the ground
or a cross, and the drowning of many
if it called from the resting places of
our brethren by the abbey. Of course
it is of no consequence to us at all
if it called from the south, for that means
a sickness or wolves among the herds,
and we would be on the sea . . .

Old man, in truth we are both too far gone
for a sail toward the sun's resting place,
which may only be a fool's long errand
toward the grave or beyond, and it's better
we both were tending lambs and onions
over there behind the cashel wall.

Those were my thoughts, but here's
what I said: —Tonight we'll go
sleepless and full of prayers together
on the mountain, that no one dream
a drove of pigs or a girl in a red petticoat.
Keep watch. Should one or another begin
blinking off, give him your sharpest elbow
with my blessing. We'll fast, so none upsets
the salt, and pray against seeing

the lame woman Maire Dubh cross a deathlook
with us before we enter the curragh
tomorrow morning. An unlikely event anyhow,
in fog and that far up the mountain.

All the path down to sunlight I prayed through
a mist so woolly no bird, sheep, shepherd,
birdcall, rare-colored stone, or calf
was seen or heard, not even a bee
humming about the pleasures of its labor.
There were tide glints as from
an archangel's breastplate when we made the boat.

— Now, to your places! Wading in, I took the tiller.

Four trimmed their oars, and Conor cast us
off, but before I could stop him
leapt in over the curragh's left side.

— The devil from us if that doesn't call
a halt to it, Owen cried. At the oars
they all four sat openmouthed
and round-eyed as those stone heads
that sit staring about our hills.

— Bruising and breaking of bones on
whoever lifts a leg over that rail!
I bellowed into their faces. We are
going down this creek!

And so whatever way clouds went, we went.
Call it cracking a knee to God's power
if you like, since nowhere
is it more manifest than on that ocean,
but what were our choices when
no curragh can sail head to the wind
anyway? Islands waited, one
under every cloud that stood
building on itself as though moored,
while all the other clouds rushed on.

When gannet Christ, walking a wave
of air, claps wings and spears through
your ribs for your soul, you are less
than a clutch of fish bones
washed up on the world, with no
earthly purpose save to deny the lit
eye of a woman and the poured-milk
turn of her neck. Neither hills like
paps of Danu nor fields potent with mares
nor tables buckling under spread
feasts provoke you, but grip, hilt,
and blade, the cross is a sword
turned against this life, and you dream
in your stone beehive of islands:
shag-defended heights backlit by evening;
rocky stacks; mere humps supporting
washed-up mats of scraw; landfalls of
sheep fat as cattle; egg islands
where, flapping your arms, you drive birds off
and fill your baskets for the change
of diet; treeless anvil shapes without
anchorage; tern-swarmed beaches; skerries;
a narrow stretch between rockfaces
riddled with caves, fast water reeled over
by a dinning stir of gulls, gannets,
puffins, guillemots, skuas—and then
that island you never dream, the one
you'll know only when you wade ashore
and feel, among the bindweed and reddening
ferns, in the silence of lichen-flowering
stones, like a trespasser on some
lump of everlastingness. You'll never know
unless you drop that quill and sail, my boy.

We met no monks offering bread, no otters
that led us to clear wells, but scavenged
winkles on what strands we could,
dropped bait and fished, trolled fish
when a fulmar trailed our wake. One day
far on in summer, in fog so thick you couldn't

find your eye with your thumb, we heard
voices in antiphon traveling across water,
monks singing, but as we closed on them
more as if folk had convened on a festival day,
each agreed to sing his favorite air
at the same time. Nearer, it turned anarchy:

— The punished dead, howling and slobbering around
with Pilate and Judas, enisled here for eternity,
Owen cried, churning his ancient hands.

That old man could talk the sea up a duck's arse,
God rest him, even fed the others once
when we ran up on an island bejumping
with rabbits that the poor creatures
were witches. He was handy to whistle up
a breeze when we were becalmed
as swans in a lough, but sometimes his
delusions found soft nests in his brothers'
minds. The singing that chilled us so
came from a rock pile where the seals
hauled out to try their human voices.
Owen sang back, of course, as we passed,
nothing I could sing you now,
but a kind of babbling a child
in his bath in the stream might make,
sounds you might like to hear, but nothing
in any tongue I know about,
until their music faded off our stern.

Don't mis-hear an old man and set it down
that we came across souls out there.
They were as surely seals as those
radiant blobs we sometimes plowed
our way through in the dark were jellyfish,
not souls. Seals, I said, not souls.
But you may have heard—nor would I
be putting an egg in your cowl,
for I tell you truly—that on the north leg
of our voyage sometimes an island floated

on the sky. You could see a band of light
between it and the water, and if it was
a cloud it was one with brown hills on it,
and grass above the shoreline. This
we pursued for days without reward,
since we never seemed to gain on it,
perhaps because it traveled faster than
the curragh. Though when I thought about it
afterwards, how would we get up on it
if ever we caught it? Such sights would knock
you dead, it seems like, until you see
the next thing. One morning when Cernan
was on watch, he shook me from sleep.

— You'll never believe this one, Brendan.
There on the sky, another island! Floating
upside down, its peak dangling like
a blue turnip over the waves! By your face
I can see you believe I'm doing the leg pull
on a poor boy too long in the scriptorium.
Not so. You know how its body joins
the two wings of a butterfly? Imagine
two islands then, attached at their bases,
or one doubling itself, up in the air!

In those far waters things better than
miracles appear, as though to prove
the world can supply whatever
a wandering mind might devise. One day
a brother cried from the bow
that a curragh was approaching.
Who else could have crossed that far, daring
the North beyond flaming mountains, and now
returning in trouble? She rolled too severely
for conditions, at times laid over
on one cheek, the bow lifting sometimes
as though a following sea had boarded,
swamping and righting herself as she came.

— Prepare to take her people off, I shouted,
and the crew moved to the rail. She passed us
to starboard, a chunk of hull-shaped
groaning ice, that's all. Astonishments
everywhere. Here will be the head of
a swimming horse, there a man on a rock,
gesturing like some poet spouting off
at court for an extra cupful, even as
he wobbles and sinks in a field
of minor lumps like rafts of fowl at rest.

Had I in the flesh the ice cattle I've seen
through mist, I'd be king of all Munster;
Bishop of Rome if I ruled over half
the ice clochans and oratories we outsteered
while our hull plowed the slush mumbling
and crackling against it, at times sounding
like an invisible host whose boundaries
we had violated, muttering one long
threat against the boatskin
as we steered among the statues,
poling them off our bows. White
in the distance, towered and fortified,
a dwelling place shone, seeming to draw
all sunlight to itself. This could be
that island, was my thought.

— What king's rath might that be, Diarmuid wondered
aloud, of such bright stone?

Owen I kept my eye on, ready to clap
his gob shut, as well he knew
by the look of him.

— Let us hope those who live there are Christian men,
said Martin, who had abjured all battles forever.

Its nearness proved another trick of that sea,
since all the day and into the next
we chased it without seeming to advance,

as when for the first time you sight the Rock
of Patrick and set out for it, only to learn
that the plains of Tipperary weren't made
to pleasure your feet. Nearer, we dropped sail
and drifted in such brilliance as
we had never seen. That whiteness drew
all light from surrounding waters,
blackening them as if to isolate
its own strangeness and underline
its silence. As with sheer coastal walls
that break rollers to nothings of froth
and bubbles, such monsters loom on
the mind and stagger balance.

Wrapped in cloaks, hooded, frozen
in a silence of our own, we stood with
hands clamping the rails against such
malignant loveliness. Over the ruins
of portals, cliffs, towers and melting
bridges, glazed dunes—for this too
was ice—colors slipped and played.
Fragilest blues. From vast interior
halls, greens fiercer than any bush
or tree's. Sapphires. Crystals.
Violent emeralds on undersea ledges,
all reflecting upward onto walls
and ceilings. Streams broke from above
and fell in rills to the ocean.

— Let us pull around this island awhile,
I said, and see what we can of it.

With Conor at the bow for floating ice
or shelves that might slice the skin,
we rowed within a few boat-lengths of it.
It gave off cold as well as lights, its face
here blue as June, there greeny white,
with darker greens under the dripping
overhangs, and sea ripple glittering it
everywhere in grottoes, under bridges,

a music of light on a vast smashup of
towers and caves, galleries and walls.
Whale-nosed juts bearded with icicles
protruded through in places.

— We'll go in here, I ordered at a wide
breach in the ice, for I saw that we could
bring the boat about in a baylet there
if no way through appeared.

— Father! several gasped.

— Have we come so far to turn away from
this? I roared, and took an echo
off the walls that shook me. Then
quietly I reminded my sons how
our hearts had brushed the rough skin of
eternity while a white-browed whale
cruised the vessel, his nose full of the smells
of sheep grease and ourselves. That time
I was killed with terror the while myself
until the beast dropped off our track,
and tempted to cry out to Manannan
or the Daghda, anyone but the Mother of God.

Many's the time, quaking under my cloak
like a calf who knows he's appointed for meat,
I admonished my brothers for their fear
and accused their faith while my own
turned thin as mist on a wall
and my resolve melted like snow off ditches.
Worse, at times I was afraid I'd revealed
my doubts to that sea-keeping boat.

So let us not have it that all the night
my mother thrashed in her blood to give me
to this world, the woods behind our rath
flamed in sign of my selection and by
daylight not a leaf's edge was singed—
nothing like that if you believe your soul
hangs by the single thread of the truth.

That sea is the lid of hell, and wore
an old face on its first morning.
In your ugliest night on a stone floor
you can't dream what's down there: squid
so great our whole community couldn't
stuff one in our oratory; fish
all swollen head, tall as you and four times
your bulk; lumps with fins; mouths
you could drive a donkey through; wide,
flat, winged things with eyes on their backs
and tails like oxen. Things you'd think
crawled from the Cave of Cruachan, but
I'll tremble you with them no more.
Instead I'll tell you a psalm I made
after many a sea with the ghost
of a mountain in every wave:

Doctor of our hearts, now we are as
murderers cast adrift, and would
gladly change vessels with sailors
on some glassy tide, who see
beneath them the boar-headed,
swallow-tailed ones turning bellies
pale as the drowned toward them,
and ones like swollen chestnut husks
and pincered, and other ribbony ones,
many-legged, tusked, lugworms
a weakening mind magnifies. For now
you raise a black wind from the north,
or send against us a gray west wind,
and we long for the barking of a fox
from a field's threshold after
first nocturn. Openmouthed on the edge
of every wave, we are lifted toward heaven.
Then—as our bellies drink our souls
like liquid fire—dropped
to a narrow glen. The light is
in turmoil, and our wits are useless
as cups of thrown water. We stagger this
way and that, take hold like men

by drink taken hold of and cry out
in our trouble, and hope down into the oak,
which groans for its roots again.
Each stringer of ash, bound ankle and wrist
in thongs, is a captive without reprieve,
crying out for the north side of
the mountain and a thrush at its berries.
The tree our saws drew the least
scantling from was seeded by Your hand,
and the oak's heart in our rails.
Even the ox hides we tanned in pits
of oak bark and stitched
with threads of flax, and wool grease
we slathered on our sheep-smelling hull
to keep the sea out. Therefore
our boat is from Your hand, *is*
Your right hand under us when we forsake
every heart-softening face—our white
martyrdom—for the emptiness of this
seal pasture where every angel-haunted
abbey stone sinks out of memory
and the salt blears consolations of
heather and harebell, things grown
large in our eyes. Clench Your fingers
in each stitch of flax as You did
in the roots when the weed flowered
blue against darker, wind-worked loughs,
for our mast whips sky, and our sail
is a fleeing rag. As You put breath
in the ox, breathe now with our
sea-trampler flexing its ribs to fit
water, Your eyes quick for the first
drips from faults the warblefly made
when this beast-boat plowed our fishless
fields, for we sail from bowl to bowl,
dragging the world with us, uphill
in all directions while our souls
touch bottom, longing for meadow-quiet
and a sea reflecting stars, not this
wave-beheading wind wherein the steersman

dares not look astern, but hangs like
a bug on a straw, and petrels creep
up the sides of the water.

We rowed into that cavern, then on
to a second. But for icicles plipping
and clear rills pattering down
it was quiet, the surface mild.
We moved through a honeycomb of ice,
chamber opening to chamber, each with its
own arrangement of those greens and blues.
Above, a sky swept of clouds. At every turn
I expected we'd be thwarted, ice arches
and walls closing so we'd have to take her
stern first out the way we came
and bring her about in a roomier vault.
But cavern after cavern appeared for us.

— Look. At the bow Conor pointed to a span
we were about to pass beneath.

What a thud to my heart! Two yellow eyes
up there watched us, unblinking,
bright as lamps in the ice.

— What do you make of it? I said,
once I had returned to myself.

— Now you have brought us to the silver castle
behind the north wind, where souls
are conducted after death, screamed Owen at me.

I hadn't recalled dying, I was about
to tell him, or ask if he'd drunk salt water
or seen the Black Pig, anything to draw
that poison from his mind with laughter,
and settle the crew, when something
up there took wing and carried those eyes off
with it, no doubt from Owen's noise,
and slipped across to settle on a further
ledge, leaning a little as it studied us.

— A bird, I said. Some big owl, I'd guess.

— But it's white! protested Owen.

— Well, it's white and it looks like
an owl, so I'd say it's an owl. *Big* white owl.
Why not call it down with one of your
fine songs?

Cernan and the others shook at this, with
laughter and relief, and the bird
pumped off soundlessly to another height,
turning its demeanor on us again,
more flustered than anyone but Owen,
whose face hung red between fury
and abashment like some boy's.

We were closer to land than I thought,
since there wasn't a lesser bird or mouse
an owl could live on there, but to take
the slack from a long rope, that bird
stayed with us as though on a tether
until we picked our way to open sea
on the farther side. Soon a wind for the south
banged into our sail. I missed that
caverned waste and its yellow-eyed spirit
when coastlines poked through the gray monotonies
we engaged later, and then concealed their forms.

God mend your head if you believe
I can reckon those distances or render them up
in days. As the flying bird can't hatch her eggs,
so bailing from one day through another,
chipping ice one-handed off the bow
while spray dashes it back on—
keeping her off bold shores the while—
crosses a spear with a sword
in a man's bones, cracks or flattens
his hours till day and night are one,
which in that North they are: at midnight

I have picked lice off my shirt up there
as handily as at noon. What a man
on the water wants is stars after sunset,
and to see ahead what's there
before dealing with it closely, not
a single evergreen leaning east from
a surf-bashed tumble of rocks, then gone
in mist, and again a red-faced cliff
closed over and shifted about and dragged out
further along. And don't be putting it down
in your thorny script that I foresaw
what was coming before we ever crossed horizon
to it. Any old hand knows mare's tails
on a blue-greeny pale sky mean big winds
in the offing. Same for a sunset the color
of whin blossoms, or a ring around the moon.
Ugly bottom creatures coming up for air
mean ugly weather, too, and an oily sea
that sets my joints to stabbing.

What islands we found, we found. Nameless,
unpeopled, without magical springs
except the luck of sweet bubbling water
sometimes, among cress and good roots
that let us graze awhile when we were ready
to drop, our strength poured out in our bailers,
and hollow from hours at the oars. May I not
give you scandal in saying that what fasts
we could we kept, but the day of the week's
the first land gear jettisoned out there.
Slack water bags enforced our fast days,
and provisions with seas washing in their sacks.

When we could we feasted, knowing thinner
days could be at hand when they would,
our cauldron going above Cernan's charcoal pan,
the fishheads given first to him as smith.
There were island grapes like undersized
pebbles at times, enough for a tight belly,

but keep miracles out of it. Don't edify those
grapes to the girth of apples. Day by day
the mist warmed so our cloaks were left aside
more and more, and stone-block islands
passed us by, risky for running a curragh up to.

As to the matter of this finny delusion
which I see you've given a name—
this Jasconius. This sleeping whale
you've written I let my brothers
tie the boat up to, build fires upon,
and celebrate mass on its back, returning
to it every Easter—I won't allow us
dressed up in nonsense that denies
simple sense as well as truth.

What might sound good in Rome makes me out
the witless navigator. A whale's back
is spotted, scarred-over where it isn't
barnacled, and looks nothing like
any land or stone I've set foot on, nor
is its flesh consistent enough to be mistaken so.
You're too long under this roof and need
constant airing if you think you're improving
anything with such elaborations.

Would I risk our hope of keeping from the waves
that way? No dead whale, either. Even then
it would be a stinking landfall no sailor
would get near, let alone anchor on.
What with sharks ripping gobbets off its pelt
so he'd barely get his soul back over the rail
with him, and seabirds picking it over
for a year or so, feasting it down to bones,
there'd barely be room for a wren
to step around on it. Though I'm in a tight
clutch with the years, I go back on
the clear-skied track of my thoughts,
so no more miracles, no dreaming whales
and no gryphons, either.

unless things got so we were down
at the end of sense and into each other's faces.
Best in a sea-drift curragh to think of
all that brine and overlook what you can,
walk away from it in your mind, lest it infect
and you end trying the blasphemy of walking
away from it on water like some moorhen. That'd be
your miracle if you could pull it off.

Only think of each man memorizing the same
five faces over and over, week on,
week off, wrinkle and wart and black tooth
until beards and hair thicken and spread
and blessedly obscure them. The same five
voices as month piles up on month and years
collapse with the weight of them. There's
no escape on curraghs, not even to ease
your bowels. Not even in sleep, where
you'll hear, "Diarmuid, would you get your
blessèd elbow out of my blessèd mouth!"

And believe me or don't, it's worse when
there's no dirty weather to keep heads off
fleabites and the screaming bilge reek.
When the wind's fair, it's never fair enough
but they'll be thinking with their bellies
on fresh mutton joints and feast-day cups,
and the taller worries build, the softer
the abbot speaks, and doesn't dare turn
a sharpened word against one or another's
sea skills. You know when a brother
breaks wind and nobody yells, "Beware aft!"
that your crew's in trouble.

But did I never tell you of our run
to Inishdhugan for the clay, and of
Dhugan himself, that hard, unbelieving man?
Not long from this land here the boat's
full complement of fleas discovered us,

despite our regular dippings of the flesh
in salty coves and river mouths.
Some they enjoyed more than others,
and those had from them constant generous
rings around their wrists, ankles,
necks even, thick as king's-gift torques.

— What sort is this Dhugan? I'd asked Owen,
who suggested that since we'd be passing
anyway, we put in at his island
for this clay he had. A handful sprinkled
round would drive all vermin over the rails
to the sea like Gadarene swine, he promised.

— A wee, scarce man, Dhugan is, he said,
and one to be cagey with, for he'll take
no gift for his clay, though it has the power.

And sure enough, when we made landfall,
off on the end of a promontory
we found his walled place. A couple of
old wives skulked around among his stones
and sheep, and the great man himself
sat out to the sun before his hut,
cracking a pile of limpets, a withered fellow
grown but to my shoulder, of questionable age,
whether venerable or whitened early
from a profligate life I couldn't say.

— Remember, Owen whispered, he can't be accosted
in a trifling manner. Let me try.

— In the name of Balor the One-Eyed, give me
some clay! he called out, stepping forward.

Did I tell you this was that same island
where Balor dwelt in those old stories?
Anyway, this Dhugan picked a limpet
off the heap and eyed it all over.

— What clay would that be? he asked, never
looking up even to count the extent of us.

— Your Honor's wonderful earth that a mere
fistful sends the rats hurrying from
the grain's vicinity, and clears boatloads
of lice off the premises.

— No clay I know of has the qualities
of that, Dhugan replied. It was barely
a mutter, delivered sideways.

— Sir, I said, thrusting my face into it,
I am Brendan, Abbot of Clonfert,
and these are five of my brethren.
We are sailing the seas for an island
proper for monks to contemplate God upon,
away from the traps and giddy toys
that pilfer the earthly time of men.
We beg a little of your clay to cleanse
our curragh of lice and fleas,
and offer in its stead our prayers
for your soul and its approaching journey.

— That is a thought too deep for me to wade in,
he said. But answer me this, if you can:
Why, if you're serving this God of yours,
for so you say, doesn't He send these bugs off
with a mere wave of His hand?

— It is not our business to question His ways,
I answered, and not a little too smoothly,
I might admit to you here, so I feared
I'd botched our chances for the clay, then turned
on myself at the thought I was allowing
this runt of the human litter to have his
play with me. I'd sooner be good grazing for
the vermin than cross more words with him,
I was about to tell him, when he spoke up again.

— Well, riddle me this then. I move
what cannot move itself. Though none can
see me, all bow down to me. What am I?

— God! one of the brothers whispered behind me.

— Yes, God! the others encouraged.

— Almighty God, I answered smiling at
the thought I'd cornered him now.

— The wind, he answered with a smirk.

— It could as well be true of the one
as the other, Cernan spoke up.

— Not if there is no other, said this
pointy-eared pagan dwarf, and at that
I took another step forward.

— You are singularly starved for imagination
if you truly believe what your mouth
just uttered, I said. Cernan laid a firm
hand on my arm to stay my anger.

— Well, answer me this then. I'm gray
some places, and blue, and red, and other
places green. When I die I do not die,
but make many more faces that were met
in me when I was one, who now am many.

— The sea, Cernan whispered in my ear.

— Try the soul! It must be the soul,
I heard Diarmuid behind me.

— A great host in battle. This from Martin.

— This time you have built false leads into it,
I told Dhugan straight to his pebbly eyes.
There's no such thing on all the earth. Now
it's "yes" or "no" to a bit of your clay,
and we'll be off.

He bent and picked a stone from a pile at hand.
I was ready to topple on him when
he smashed it down hard on another
so it broke to pieces of all manner of colors,
even those he'd put into his riddle.

— The answer is, this stone. Who lacks
imagination now? And might a solid man
like yourself be capable of the Salmon Leap?

My crew was sniggering at my back, not
all of it directed at this convoluted fellow.
I shrugged by way of saying I was
through with him, which he interpreted as
asking for a demonstration.

— It goes like this, he said, and laid his
ropy body flat down on his back, arms at his sides.

— The Salmon Leap! he announced, then curved
himself upward in a flash, so he was on his feet.

— Without bending your knees, he explained,
then dropped back down and showed us again.

One by one my brothers stepped forward
and performed the movement, each with
a measure of success I won't go into here,
all but Owen and myself. He wants to use us
awhile for his own beguilement, I'd decided.
Stuck on this island and not a praying man,
his sports were harmless, surely.

He ducked into his hut and came out quick.
Now we'll get the clay, I thought.

— One last trial, for certain, he said.
Stand this egg on its end and I'll
give over the clay.

It was coming on afternoon and I wanted
water under us before night was above us,
so stepped quick up and took the egg
in my palm, then went to a flat stone
on the wall and took the egg between thumb
and finger and set it fat end downward.
Need I say it rolled in a circle

until I trapped it again, and that each
brother repeated the situation? Get ready,
I cautioned myself, for next Dhugan'll
be breaking one end and sitting it in itself.

— Sure nobody who's come here yet can do
that one, Dhugan admitted, nor did he try himself.

— But wait and I'll get you the clay, he said.
No one's to follow.

Over the hill behind his hut at a trot
he went, looking back every three steps or so
to see we weren't on his track.
There's an island of speckled cursing stones
out there, so many no one ever counted
them twice but he got the different total.
Round and egg-shaped they are, and some
with carvings. You turn them left to right
for a good journey, and right to left,
against the path of the sun, to curse somebody.
They say if your curse is unjust it returns
on you like a stick with a bounce in it
tossed at a wall. Could we have found
that island I'd have risked it and turned
every pebble against that stringy little heathen
I'd prostrated my dignity to. The man was
mean as a stoat and three or four times
as cute, and not a louse or flea
swam for its life after we'd spread his dirt
about our hull. Nor would it surprise me
if that stuff wasn't the cause that
they seemed to double their coupling so more
climbed about on us than there are sheep
on summer mountainsides. It was no cure either
against those stinging bugs that flew at us
in the North, big as frogs and thick as
chaff the flail raises. Crawled over
and chewed on, it all'd make you wonder
just who the world was made for exactly.

Now as to your island of smiths,
let's bring it back down to earth and say
we passed a burning mountain or two
up there in the North, smoking away like
the turf was blazing good inside, then
roaring and sending up splashes of it so tall
its flaming sods sizzled the ocean about us
until we cleared away. We heard no anvils,
and no hairy men ran out and tossed fires
at us with tongs. These are what drink concocts
in the heads of old mariners whenever
landfolk can be seized by the earlobes
and held to hear them out, and are thus
unworthy of a monk's quill. Boat life taxes
men with long silences, and no crew loves
a windy comrade, therefore the natural
leaning toward ornament on shore. I've heard
such stories increase tenfold in color
and wonders with each retelling,
so what starts out a sprat
betimes gets inflated whaleward.

But there *is* a kind of fever that
can overtake a man after rolling long
on untenanted waters. It's not that he feels
strangely, but what he sees, which seems
always to be what he needs most. Without
warning and before he can be stopped,
a young brother's been known to get up,
walk forward to the bow and over, declaring
a woman there has given him the bashful look.

In my own case the fever began with
a jacksnipe baaing like a goat, impossible
out there. Then in clean daylight I saw
this very cashel wall, stone for stone on the sea,
and behind it our oratory with its west door
and its window slot set eastward, all these
clochans, the graveyard and monks' garden,

so real I might have plucked a cabbage leaf
to chew on. Brother Donal at his plow
raised a clutter of worm-hunting gulls
along the furrow at his back. I knew
his face. Meanwhile hawthorn whitened
all the world, heather wrestled with swine smell
and clover and the bread oven. I heard
wind clashing branches together where those oaks
lean away from the coast, and blackbirds.

Cernan and Owen caught me and held me down,
and in my tears I knew it wasn't the island
out ahead I wanted, but stone-ringed
Clonfert here behind us. The monk in harness
to his Lord, facing down the furrow of his duty.
Not this endless salt-plowing after every
wink of light at its edge. So when we shook
the fogs off and found that island,
I didn't go ashore, and forbade the others.
Tempted, as you'll see, but afraid the place
might keep me, that I'd never again hear our
sweet bell calling me to prayer a windy night.

Make note that I was the only one
who saw and heard what I saw and heard,
and can somewhat understand that the others
might doubt my word, given that they'd
had to take hold of things until I put myself
back together, though hadn't I led them
to that place without harm—Diarmuid excepting,
of course, whose poor fortune casts no mud
on anyone's over-assurance or neglect.
It was Martin and Conor, here at home,
scattered the tale I'd lost my sand
at the last of it and wouldn't go ashore
out of fear, so hatched the events
I'm about to lay out for you.

You know the way a bog-stained stream mingles
with a clear one? Between matins and prime

the night's like that—diluted with morning
so another twilight tricks the eyes.
Then it's better to trust your ears alone.
The boat laid-to, the sea quiet,
what I heard was a rush of air like
a shearwater whizzing past, then
a rustle like wings folding.

Visible or not, something was there
in the cockpit a few feet away,
in the stillness deepened by the sighing boat
and my crew snuffling and snoring
under sheepskins. Think of it. I might have
reached across and touched it—or him.
I didn't, though calm in my heart.

— Brendan.

— You know me then?

— Though you crossed by the skill of twelve
hands alone, I hung nine masts above you
all the way from the other side.

Oh that's a comfort, thought I, now that
it's over. Then hoped he hadn't power
to listen inside as well as out.

— Yesterday, he went on, when this landfall
seemed only a low blue cloud stretched
across the horizon, sighted on the moment
of each crest, lost with each drop to a trough,
before it rooted itself in the sea and every
weed patch and tern homing to it made it true,
before it separated to leafy woods above white dunes .

Tell me what I already know, I was
thinking, when he took a new tack.

— A long, starless night will drop
down the northern way that brought you here,

island to island as the traveler uses
stepping-stones to cross a stream. Men of
the bays, flying the hawk's banner:
red for the blood of your brothers-to-be,
staining pasture and strand; black for
the burnt stones of abbeys. The anchorite's bell
will ring out fainter and fainter on oceanic
silence, while thick-handed strangers fondle
the staff of Patrick and fair women,
and brute gods enthrone your altars. Then,
iron-chested ones sailing out of sunrise
to envenom the cup of peace. Sly as the goldwork
on a warrior's brooch, the little kings
will entangle son with father, brother against
brother. Where towers like dragon's teeth
remind the land a thousand years, bishops
will hunt the red deer instead of souls.
Then Christian bones, starved and staring,
walking the bogs and mountains, stripped of
everything from lambkin to mother tongue, even
the dirt that might clothe their rest.

I thought to waken Brother Owen to see if
he could unravel this jabber for me,
but feared this one's presence might set
the teeth of death in the old man.

— You seem bottomlessly endowed
with dire riddles, I told him. But say it
plain, since I'm long on years and won't
play what children's games I won't.

— When these things come to pass, your people
will need the sanctuary of places like this.
I say "your people" though none on your island
thinks himself part of a race, but only
a member of some narrow kingdom at war with
every other, and therein is the cause of this
coming nightfall—petty alliances with strangers,
the daughter sold in marriage for personal gain,
revenge of piddling, half-imagined slights.

— That is a sad truth. But tell me,
what place is this?

— Call it the land beyond the wave.
You are the first I've led here, but others
will sail across centuries to it.

— I praise God for it.

— Well you might, considering that lifelong
you have turned a cold face to the creation
He set you in to love and find Him through.
This world was complete without you, man,
or any of your kind. There is no reason
for you or anyone, and nobody's worthy
of this world, yet all whimper against it
as you do, wanting blue eyes if theirs
are brown, or a smaller nose or waist.
Half your race is walking around with
stiff nostrils as though each step sunk them
deeper in manure, while others figure—
oh the constant figuring! Here's one
over here figuring how to barter a field
for more bullocks to swap for a larger field
while that one over there's calculating
how to market his daughter to the son
of the other with all the bullocks
without throwing an extra field into
the bargain. Meantime this third fellow
with no bullocks or fields is looking
for ways to get the other two spitting
in their palms and shaking on the arrangement
so he can secure a field from the one
and a few bullocks for it from the other.
Go down to the strand and you'll find
another waving a stick above a heap
of shells, as if they'll turn gold
and shiny stones if he can only get
the motion right—and this the one time
they'll walk the world!
Never do they account that purely from

their Creator's largess they're here, not
from any excellence of their own.

He was in a fine ruffle. Best not to cross
talking points with this one.

— And your own little pile of shells is
that you've had both eyes on eternity
so long you've never thought to thank Him
for the marvels of your own creaturehood.
Smell it, man! Take a deep breath
for once in your life without fearing
you'll spring a rib through a lung
just for falling in love with the world.

Like a swung thurible or cauldron stirred,
breath of the simmering land
passed over the ship. Warmth the sand stored
in every grain, released on the night breeze,
tangible as a sail bellied all day
to the sun. Cedar. Pine resins drawn out
by the heat. A hint of clay under salt-blown
roses, then dankness rising from fallen leaves.
Nothing like mild Clonfert, but
such excess in my nostrils as almost
to knock me on my stern-end.

— Here where no man behind a wall
has dropped his ear in on his neighbor's
business yet, for a time the creation
will please its Maker with original
birdsong again. He drifts in wild-flower
pollen across your bow and strikes
tendrils from seeds and rain from clouds.
He is there in this startling vine fragrance
and in mud flats edged with rotting fish,
in fish rot and stone damp and rockweed
baking on sand. He's the purple,
blue, and maroon of berries you'll taste
behind that shore.

— I'll taste no berries over there,
nor dip a foot in those shallows. From here
we swing this boat sunward for home.

My boldness startled me as much as him, I think.
But now the stones were tumbled
and the horse was out the breach:

— My own pile of shells, is it? Larking around
in the sky while we're down here keeping
this curragh from drinking up the ocean,
sleeping so long under wet sheepswool we've turned
reeking leather satchels bagging our own guts?
Eating in the dark so we won't see
what's already eating what we're supposed to eat?
Wondering the while when our joints will swell
and lock so fleas and lice can pick us
to the marrow without fear of being scratched?
How many call *you* Father? I never took vows
to be abbot, but I got three thousand sons
anyway, in this world and the next, and right now
the full wet weight of a drowned one sitting
here on my heart. All because I set the second stone
on the first at Ardfert, Clonfert, Inchiquin,
and twenty other places, and spent my life
talking monks into staying around each year
when the oats were ready to come in, instead of
letting them traipse off home to comfort their
poor old mothers. *You* try playing Solomon
when one brother says a Connaught man
can resurrect a ram long enough
to get the trade done, and the other says
the scrawniest cat in Connaught would walk away
from a Munster trout, and it goes to "I piss
in your ear" and back and forth to unnatural
things about the other man's sister
and from there to knife points.

Thick as my neck was in those days, this angel—
if so he was, for *now* I remembered

the Evil One on the heights with Our Lord—
this winged creature closed hands around my neck
the way a gannet wraps both feet about
its unhatched egg, and shook me off the deck.

— Say it, man! Out with it!

And I, weak as a hen who sees her future
in the pot, but thinking of this Clonfert
my delirium had spread before me on the sea,
and getting out of that one's clutches
back here to it:

> *O Lord*
> *I have loved*
> *the Glory of*
> *Your house*

NOTES

PAGE 97

Although Clonfert Abbey was located in East Galway, the monks depart from what is now Brandon Creek, on the Dingle Peninsula, Kerry.

PAGE 106

The Arctic Mirage, or Hillingar Effect, as it is called in Iceland, is created when a quantity of cloudless, motionless atmosphere stabilizes over a much cooler surface and alters the optical character of the air so that it curves the light like an enormous lens. Landmasses far beyond the horizon then appear to be within sight, floating above the horizon, sometimes upside down or one above the other.

PAGE 122

The fever Brendan experiences is usually called a calenture in sailing lore.

Balor. Balor of the Evil Eye, who was believed to have lived on what is now called Tory Island, the Inishdhugan where the monks sail for the clay. Balor's eye was so large and powerful it required four men to raise the lid. It could destroy an army with one look.

Beltane. May Day, the beginning of Irish summer, which is celebrated with bonfires.

Cashel. The stone wall surrounding the monastic property, meant in a legal sense to define the sanctuary and to serve as a barrier against intrusion.

Cave of Cruachan. The entrance to the Other World.

Clochan. A circular stone "beehive" hut.

Daghda. Literally, "Good God," a pagan deity of wisdom, whose cauldron was endlessly bountiful and one end of whose club was used to kill the living, the other to bring the dead back to life.

Mannanan. "Son of the Sea," the chief pagan Irish sea god.

Oratory. An oblong stone chapel, in shape like an overturned boat.

Rath. A circular earthwork mound inside a ditch or moat, within which an extended family lived. In stony areas, a wall with no ditch was substituted. Also called a ringfort, either sort was as much a containment for livestock as a defense against attack.

Sheep Islands. The Faroes.

Great Blue (1990)

Chickadee

The crow is only an anvil,
and the goldfinches' song
can be duplicated by rubbing
the right sticks together.
Next to yours
the blue feet of titmice
are merely a fad.

There are jays with voices
full of elbows
in my world, too,
dragoons on leave,
who appear to have molted
all the way to their head points.

But you, minimal wingbeat,
you're there, not there:
the economy of your arrival
puts a whole squad
of evening grosbeaks to shame.

I believe that other puritan
was looking at you when
he first thought, "Beware of
enterprises that require
new clothes."

I've believed in your way
since that evening
the owl sat
waiting for light to drain
into dusk, and you
flew straight in

and, seeing him there,
at the last instant
dipped up just enough,
and taught me
the duende of chickadees.

Seals in the Inner Harbor

Ducks, at first, except they didn't
fly when we rounded the jetty
and swung into the channel,
didn't spread panic among themselves,
peeling the whole flock off the water,
but followed, popping under
and poking up as if to study our faces
for someone, their eyes rounded still
by the first spearing shock of ice,
or amazed to find our white town
here again, backed by a steeple
telling the hours in sea time.
Their skeptical brows seemed from a day
when men said a green Christmas
would fill this harbor with dead
by February. We left them hanging
astern at world's edge, afloat on
summer's afterlife: gray jetty,
water and sky, the one gray vertical
of smoke rising straight from a chimney
across the cove. We could believe
they were men who had dragged
this bottom till its shells were smooth
and round as gift shop wampum,
who never tied up and walked away
a final time, but returned for evenings
like this was going to be, thirsting
for something to fight salt off with,
needing a place to spit and plan
the rescue of children's children.

Pollen

As when a breeze
slips off the water
and crosses a headland,
and even those limp zeroes
wavelets make, fragile as
smoke rings, erase themselves
from the viscid surface,
and sails slacken,
so the air
this afternoon slackens,
and the page blurs
under your eyes
as the massive invisible
orgy of flower
quickening flower
sifts through the atmosphere,
drifts at its peak,
rose to rose,
and from roadside locust trees
birds stagger, drunk,
daring tires, kneeling in the grass.

Insistent as midges, grains
tease at your nostrils,
and you cry onto the page
for no human reason.
And if somewhere
a boy's arm breaks the chains
of this lassitude
long enough
to toss a stone at a squirrel,
that pine exploding into gold
tilts you toward sleep
lightly. You whisper
how wings and the shadows of
wings circle you,
surrounding the years.

In Egg Time

All sixty-three of his years
we've been at this circling
of the planet together, this dog
and I lapping the high school track,
going gray about the face
at about the same rate. When I
begin multiplying the minutes
by average calories burned,
he lags and cuts across
the soccer field, telling me
to ease up. Redwings are trackside
in the reeds again. May. Three males
keep us in line from three
dogwoods, while the fourth takes
the sun on his back so we can't
find him, and stays up there
till we're out of nest range.
Not like the terns next month
on Egg Island, where we'll
come close to a furious barbering
all the way down the flats.
But I'd know that collar up ahead
anywhere: killdeer, first claimant
on this field when the grass
shakes winter off. Dragging
a corporal stripe away from some
pocket of earth that's warmed
to the rounding of things, this one's
trying to lead us off stride,
a wing-fake we won't
fall for, locked as we are
in our own distraction display.

Mayflies

Years in the bottom scum
of local cow ponds,
wriggling free of former
selves, learning new ways
to breathe—till they rise
in unison before a dawn, unable
even to feed, between their brad
heads and split tail-hairs
new wings that drive
each female to charge
a wandering black cloud of
mates that looks as though
it could jam horsepower.

Under them frogs dance
and splay, tonguing air
to get up where birds
work the swarm's crackling edge
before its passion fails
to a carbon fall.

Let the great trees look down
and judge from their hill
above the school how close it comes
to the May evening
a cloud of color swirls
in that cafeteria.

Prom night: plenty inside
would tell you that school
and this one-cylinder town
are like life under water,
the whole cycle. But tonight,
trailing sherbet colors
and scents those colors might have
all over town, they seem taller
than last year, as around them
parents set off flashbulbs . . .

Here I will let analogies fail,
not say what mothers and fathers
and teachers are like,
but drop such connections into
the mind of Jimmy, town drunk,
where they will spin and grow wet,
leaves on a pool awhile,
which drift, sink, decompose as
he watches from those trees.

Summer School

Three coke bottles of your Uncle Sal's
homemade red couldn't give me back
summer, 1958, and the one glance
it took in Organic lab to scramble
my ketones with my aldehydes—
it was a little *mal occhio*, a little bit
French nun, and you were that dark
woman the disabled give up their
subway seats for, the kind
a grown man looks at only once, and
even at mass takes on the instant,
permanent face of loss for.
In your mother's living room, behind
your father's garage, barefoot on
evening grass where insects zigging
too near our colliding particles
crackled and burned out, kissing you
was like sampling a little of everything
your *nonna* devised in her summer kitchen
below the stairs. Those nights
I stumbled home through the changed
streets, drunk on your breath
and mumbling in tongues, saying
Cassata alla Siciliana, Pasticcio,
Zuppa di Vongoli, to lean on the back door
humming and sweating like a nervous
frigidaire, finally understanding
how your cousins might be driven
to slaughter each other in Fanotti's
and the Old Palermo, and not so much
elevating you to a pedestal
as onto the shoulders of six fishermen
to be borne through streets
where I'd pin on you
the petitions of a towering desire.
Fireworks; hangdog days spreading with
humid silences; hour of the graven
forehead and your veal marsala

arrested a moment on your mother's
screen door, a chic wall hanging.
Had we kissed just then, with that
metal between us, it would have run like
mercury through our fingers. What's worse,
Sicilian Muse, I knew you knew.

Warmth

One flick of the wrist
and heat from the baseboards
comes sneaping around your ankles
like the worthless, expensive
pet of a sycophant.
But for warmth that stands up to you
when you come in the kitchen door,
warmth tinged with coffee,
bayleaf, cloves, and stick cinnamon,
that drifts from the pot and meets you
face to face, you have to kneel
in blue, knuckle-popping cold
as in the oldest liturgy,
stiff-shouldered and shaggy
as any man any dawn, and petition
the four-legged iron belly of
the stove against the meniscus
of frost on every window. It takes
junk mail under sleeves of bark
and those shingle-thick
parings the axe sliced away
from knots tough as trolls' knees
to summon heat that tells February,
Move it! Quit dragging your heels!
and brings the hideaway milkweed bug
in his orange racing stripes
out of his log to muse at
your windows and make you wonder
who else is out there
sleeping in your woodpile.

Fog Township

It's that delicate time
when things could spill
any way, when fog
rides into the hollows,
making bays, and Cathedral
and Round Hills are
high islands. Brooks
have already churned back
into their beds to trickle
their own placid names
again, and cloud shadows
have drawn across
the landscape's lightest
moments. Now I begin
to hear something trying
to come through, a message
tapped on twigs out there:
the spring genius of this
foggy township knitting up
cable and chain to bind
the acres, among moss stitches
laying down her simple
seed and fern stitch,
complicating the landscape
a pattern a day: daisy
stitches and wild oats,
berry knots interspersed
with traveling vine
and dogwood. Her needles,
cut from oak tips,
click like sparks fired
across a gap, and I
imagine her crouched on
a stump, hair wet, pulling
April back together.
But for the lethargy that's
floating in this fog

in nets so fine they can't
be seen, I might walk around
out there until I meet her,
or scare off the jay
who's chipping for sustenance
along a pine's gray limb.

Fall Squashes

The lettuce long bolted to exotic
headdresses, beanleaf riddled to ribs,
I find them beneath tatterdemalion
leaves: little exclamations,
not the bludgeons of August
left on friends' carseats,
but the plants' final nudges,
green and gold, and patty pans
like the minor gears of some natural
machine—which I brush with garlic oil
and grill briefly, and eat for
themselves alone. Tasting how well
they've survived root borers and slugs,
days of blue, unmoving air,
I think back along the vine
to the first watermelon-tigered leaf,
the seed-shell riding its edge,
and beyond to the flat seed
with its journey packed in,
as deep as anything.

Great Blue

Often,
around certain backwaters
like the ponds behind the oyster shacks,
I hope for a heron,

and sometimes I'm granted
that wood-silver,
crooked-stick, channel-marker effect
of the loosened neck,

and that silence, humped like
an overburden of experience,
the weight it hauls in flight
from river to pond above a highway

when I look up at the mere
abstract silhouette *bird* but am taken
by the dragged beat of wings

translucent at their tips,
and the cocked spurs trawled behind,
and have to swerve to hold the lane.

But I never expected it this morning,
Mother, on the wall of this room
you share with strangers:

the Egyptian sign for the generation
of life, its wisp of feather
hairlike off the nape, among the old
in their own humped solitudes.

Reason, that chain-store item,
can deny this forever, but that bird
shadows us, at key moments is there,

its gumped-up look guarding justice,
longevity, the journey
of the good and diligent soul.

My Grandmother Steals
Her Last Trout

(DONEGAL, 1884)

Last night a star followed
the crescent moon, trailing it
west, motif for a journey,
and this morning, skirts tucked,
wading the brook she dammed
with turf, she soothes feet unused to
the boots she's been breaking in
for wear in a Boston kitchen.

All her signs say water.
In its jostling she hears
brothers and sisters
lark in the sleeping loft.
She knows each shallow pool
below her dam, each stone
with a fish in its
shadow. Quick hands
scoop another trout up the bank.
She scrambles after, looks the field
round for the bailiff, slips
it flipping into the fattening
bag: this is demesne land.

F, like the scythe's handle;
T, for the handle of the spade;
Y, the rake's handle:
with the shank of a clay pipe
she has practised her letters
on flagstone. She is Mary Ann,
and she's ready. Below, in the village,
they're baking oaten bread.

Three times to the oven
means loaves for a long sailing.
Last Hallow Eve, blindfolded,

she bypassed the plate heaped with
clay, escaping her death,
and the ring's plate, meaning
marriage, and set her hand
in the plate bearing water.

Donegal

Bog cotton and whin. A stone
gets up and is a black-faced
sheep. Between a fog
and a rain, mist hangs,
vaporous as the lace
across these *Gaeltacht* windows.

Now I understand
why treelessness and
bog that keeps brown water
are in me like a code,
Grandfather. These crossroads
where I try to place you
could be on Iceland
or the moon, and all
I hoard of you won't fill
the shallowest socket
rain has worked in limestone.

Were you to stand under
a signpost here, translating
An Clochan Liath for me,
I wouldn't know you
as I don't what flowers
ascetically out of these rocks.
But as if the dead
merely exile themselves
to wander with the sheep,
I still expect you here,
maybe among the offspring
of some O'Donnell chief,
hiding out another century.

Which of these golden beaches
curving west toward Massachusetts
held you at the Cape
long after summer? What lough
do I render to your name;
which crossing of three roads
and red-haired children?

There was a Viking back there
in our turfpile, behind a child's
version of your face, and some
of us are redheads still.
But to say how the world began
where sheep lie down for
the journey into quartzite,
I will have to learn that single
jog of the head
men use to speak paragraphs
on the weather and the hard road
around here, where a lark
goes up each morning,
singing to penetrate the sun.

Hearing Irish Spoken

Later I'd understand how it put
the Atlantic west of them
again, kept places where scraggly grass
prevented the stones from ganging up
the way they did in Boston. On the top
rear porch of a triple-decker,
it tied them to whitewashed farmsteads
splashed with slurry, cowprints
baked in mud by the blue summer air.
All through the distant thwack and roar
of baseball at Glendale Park,
the Saccos voluble at their supper
next door, it ran like water
steady a thousand years from a limestone
lip, plaited itself through bogs
that absorbed roadsigns in English,
ran with watery sunlight after days
of rain. How Anna McCarron rejected
Donal Rua and he went out to Australia;
how a bachelor's money is never lucky.
Time left them to themselves,
left them themselves celebrating
an outlaw tongue. I stood at the twilit
meeting of their knees and voices,
wondering if it meant some failing in me.

A Holy Well

I'll drink if I can find it,
but in Ireland now
these springs are unattended,
their wallsteads fallen
into pasturage. Signs
that led me a quarter-mile
beyond the new suburb
leave me here, with the saint's
roofless church open as
a dory to the sky. Outside
and in, centuries of the dead,
mounds and depressions
the sheep are sexton to.
The farmer, almost as modern
as I am, wears a face
passionless as a board
when I climb his wall by
a stair of jutting stones,
one eye out for his bullocks
and one for the minor
penance of their droppings.
Sourney, Boden, Gobnait—these
saints with small-town names
never walked on water. But
the mice trusted them,
and they knew which branch
to tap the ground with
so a spring bubbled up
to plump a child
from a rickle of bones.
Somewhere in this unmown grass
there may be a pagan water hole
that got christianized, where
I'll drink knowing brand names
haven't cured me, loving
the nerve of a common place
that's holy. If this one
isn't muffled in chloroplasm,

if there's a fish circling
its depths like a golden torque,
I'll drink to the miraculous
ordinary: a wren entrusting
an egg to a saint's hand.

The Apple Trees

They look twisted
because
they draw fruit from under earth
into the air,
and this overthrowing
of gravity needs
the shotputter's backward
crouch, and
the trees' every bulge
concentrating on
the pure form of the sphere,
even those knots around the eyes
that have to meet the grimace of January
face to face, that have to
endure the leaves letting go one by
one as their body-sails learn
the updrafts. So what if,
in the journey from root hair to branch,
the fruit passes through
knees and elbows and comes out
gnurled, unbalanced, nodal,
moon-dragged all one way? Don't those
tears in the heart of each apple
resolve to try it again,
over and over?

Kale Soup

The Mayflower Café, the Vets' Club on
Shankpainter Road, or maybe Cookie's Tap
before the name and linoleum
vanished and pork chops *vinha d'alhos,*
meaning "wine of garlic,"
and *ameijoas,* meaning littleneck quahogs,
got kicked off the menu. Or maybe
you tried it first from a
back-of-the-stove stockpot in some
grandmother's kitchen, a dark,
fertile root of a woman
who drove to the hill above
Race Point and sat till she sighted
the family boat hauling home
from Georges Bank. In all those places
it was the same and different, with
or without carrots, with or without
chicken or lamb left over
from Sunday, but always simmered a day
over heat so low it never
raised a bubble, and built
with plenty of this, a little
of that, some more of the other,
a text brought by heart
from the Azores, when names like
Codhina and Gaspar entered
the whalers' logbooks. Always
linguica in it, which put the oak
in the forearms of dorymen,
vinegar for the vinegar of it,
chourico for setting the otter trawls,
garlic and cumin that thickened
the blood and sent trapboats
toward sunrise and the bluefins
thrashing and cruising
in a jerry-rig of nets and stakes.
You bought a store downtown
and painted it heliotrope

to catch summer people. You called it
garbage soup and denied you ever
ate it. But some nights in autumn,
coming home, you pass through a fog
so husky with smoked pork and spices
you're gaffed by the hook
of this whole peninsula.

The Connecticut River in Flood

We were with you, of course,
though for us that America
is over, its energy
siphoned into car phones
going to Hartford.
Still, we can picture you
shoving along on your raft
with the flagpole wrenched
off a neighbor's lawn,

and it looks like
you must have pushed out
across places that never were
until the river found them,
moving at the speed
of old leaves packed deep
as mattresses,
passing water-wimpled trees
on the sunken islands,

dodging snags, watching shad
shoot upcurrent to spawn,
and those Wind River ranges
and Tetons of cloud
whose colors will turn up
in lilacs outside our windows
if Canada dries out, if this rain
ever stops. Even from here
there's a look of imminence
on those bends up ahead,

as though a flatboat might
suddenly happen, with men
dancing and telling lies
for the sheer hell of it,
fleas on a dog, hat slappers,
ring-tailed roarers
and a mouth harp calling the tune.
Or else a pirogue drifting down,

its gunwales barely above the flow,
the cat tethered near the bow
twinned in meditation
with the paddling fur trader.

But who, on our gridlocked bridges,
would hear and agree if you'd yelled
that we're all half-horse,
half-alligator until we deny it?
We were with you
in retrospect, until your raft
ground into this morning's
bullhorns and they booked you
here on page nineteen,
without asking how you happened
onto the roof of Riverpark's new gazebo.

Wampanoag Traveler: Being, in Letters, the Life and Times of Loranzo Newcomb, American and Natural Historian (1989)

Wampanoag Traveler is based on some of the surviving correspondence of the eighteenth-century American natural historian Loranzo Newcomb, a self-taught "pilgrim forager," as he styled himself, who gathered seeds, botanical specimens, and fauna for the gardens and collections of patrons in England. Although virtually nothing is known of his personal life beyond what is conveyed in his letters, he appears to have been active during the first quarter of the 1700s and to have traveled through both the northern and southern colonies while based in an area of New England inhabited by the Wampanoag tribes. I have tried to remain true to the spirit and flavor of his life, which proceeded in a time very different from ours and in the light of a worldview we can but slightly understand, in which science and superstition were interlocked and the America beyond the Atlantic coast was truly a dark continent.

B.G.

I

Now I will tell you our manner
of gardening here, which progresses
not by calendar, but by natural signals.
On a clear March night, I sight down
the Dipper's bowl for a backwards
question mark, tail of the rising Lion,
and then may be found slapping mud
from the plot into balls, squeezing
to test for water content, this before
even a single mallard clacks from
the creek, and last year's pumpkins
seem the wreckage of its quarter moons.
Then the whole plot is already staked
in my head, minus slugs, borers,
hornworms, loopers, beetles and all
that plague I forget each year
until they descend like a host of
savages to be bought off
only by a feast of this or that leaf,
and dug out of vines and stems
where they poke without welcome.
Asparagus I intercrop with parsley,
since I have discovered they agree
with one another. The latter germinates
long, and is said to go to the Devil
and back nine times ere it breaks
the soil, but I have found it mild
and without evil influence. Beans
I keep far from onions they can't
abide, and basil, which breeds
a merry heart, I grow along borders
with umbelliferous dill, whose leaves
are agreeable with fish, though of
a strength not to everyone's taste.
These strong-scented herbs, with chives
and mint, may keep a barrier against
insects, though my studies here
need more attention. Native squashes

and gourds are set when the dogwood
flowers, and tomatoes during
the mayfly hatch. This conveys somewhat
our manner of gardening. I would
continue but that in the mere telling
I grow fatigued, and must ask myself why,
yearly, I engage in it with such ardor
since I am without family. For the surety
of plenty, or the images such growth
alone provides, or because I do better
with vegetable kind than human,
no easy admission, and have come to
myself more than once knocking upon
and addressing a blue squash
of five-stone weight and pebbled like
the back of an alligator? By the time
of the Perseids, when my turnips go in
for autumn, I am as weary as some
old king fighting his battle with
the sea, down on hands and knees in that
riptide of beans and cabbage splashes,
a spume of chickweed flying over
my shoulders, wishing I had never listened
for spring peepers chiming their long,
ghostly sleighrides through the dark.

II

Six foot of mingled orange, tawny,
and black, its underside leaden,
a rattlesnake I kept for study
in an empty rum keg, thinking the vapors
would befuddle him, one morning
lay in wait under that cover when I came
with a snared chipmunk, and struck
my hand, pumping green poison in.

I knew I had only minutes, so cornered
a chicken in the yard, breaking her neck
with a quick upward jerk, and with
the selfsame knife as I had hacked
my murderer to portions, which yet rolled
and snapped along the floor as though
each worked to produce its own head,
I split the hen's belly and plunged
the insulted hand into her still-working
jellies and hot lights, whereon I swear
the thing's feathers wilted and began
dropping away.

                    That serpent I kicked
piece by piece to the hearthfire, and soon
began a splutter and popping of fats,
a whooshing of steam among the flames,
while on my hand the fowl, now black
as though itself roasted there,
stunk in a way the Devil was in the room.
It too I added to the fire, its vile smoke
offered heavenward, then wrapped the hand
with a plaster.

                    Along their routes
veins stood and flared to the elbow,
though I plunged the arm in a bucket of
vinegar and waited upon Fate. A tree
tingled and grew from the tips of my
fingers, swelling itself up my forearm

until with a razor I opened my palm
and let my own blood flow.

I rolled and steeped some days upon my bed,
waking at times to discover the arm itself
a mottled snake, its arrowhead buried
and drinking at the chambers of my heart.
In dreams and awake I was rolled in lowly places,
sumps of the deepest hollows, among the pulp
and lichens of tumbled, ancient deadfall,
cobwebbed, prickled with my own drenched bedding.

At times I even seemed to myself a tree,
toes feeling downward toward groundwater,
at my extremities these woody prongs,
scaled, soft-pithed, where juices
wended toward the terminal buds,
which were lapped over and sometimes
in my fevers flowered, blue-lipped,
orange at heart, or rosy and black-veined,
and again like gold-wormed feather dusters.

I was possessed at times with fears and watchings.
Then vermin drew near, their faces large
as my own, lights malefic in their ebony eyes,
each sentient hair distinct, their mouth parts working,
warning against ambulations into their kingdoms.

Some evenings I was settled with cooler moments,
and at dusk, from the swamp and beyond,
a surf of sound arose as from another village
in there. I could pick out some drunkard or
madwoman's denials, but not attach them
to the screech owl, and sounds like someone
hacking brush, and breaths blown across
the mouths of flasks.

                I reflected how these
mortal troubles began when I listened almost
from the cradle while the yellow rail sounded,

and a flycatcher whistled, desultory. Later
I stood hours on the threshold of that
bush world, thinking the pygmy owl's bark
a pup crying somewhere, boxing the air
at the end of its tether, and one day
entered a few feet in.

                  Now at times it seemed
I wandered unattended in landscapes where maroon
leaves of the oak formed metallic masks,
and was observed from thickets by eyes cognizant
of my passage there, and heard such chuckles,
small laughter and rattling, I imagined the mice
dicing, hands pressed on their mouths.

In the few hours of clarity vouchsafed me,
I was capable of depicting the seed vessel of
a lotus, with threatening holes
where the pips were cast, and land snails
nearby, and a rubythroat in arrested flight,
grasping a serpentine branch above
a hollowed log whose sockets menaced me.

That bird stares where a green lizard
emerges from a cover of pickerelweed,
engorging a bullfrog by the head, the frog's
feet clawing air. A green miasma ran in me yet.

III
(APPRENTICED TO THE
BIRD MASTER)

Trout for his fish hawk's clamp,
torn ducks, shrews, what a congeries
of the bloated and debrained
I gathered. Two autumns
I scaled trees Old Longabelly
couldn't negotiate, bringing
empty nests to earth, and more than once
a papery hornet's globe.

I was his retriever as well as cook
and pack beast, and drubbed enough
for all three when he was sliding in
his boozing can. Had you crossed us
on some trace, you'd have had to peel
your best eye to discover me

under skins and dangling corpses,
strapped about with sacks, hung with
the jug he replenished at every
settled turn in the road. Thus piled,
you might take me for a wandering
apothecary whilst he trotted ahead,
wheezing under his flintlock,
a clay pipe stuck in the bore.

Grog blossoms throve across his face
and he slowed day by day,
drawing more and more to parlors,
cozening benefactors with his
beaded moccasins and a wolf's tooth
at one ear, playing senex to young ladies,

betwixt times working from models
too long stale. Therefore
his later plates are without innocence
or belief: creation's exuberance
isn't in them, though hearsay

and foozling are, as where his blue
grosbeak graces a meadowlark's nest.

Hours in the dark he stared
whispering to his cup and to the fire.
Perhaps there he saw "the underground
castle of the swallows" he portrayed
in number 129. And though he led me
to riverbanks and trained my eye

for the cleanest streaks of ochre
and red earths, and forever wandered
off trail for a scrape of black lead
or pine-green clay he seemed
to know was there—which I'd crush
in the mortar cup and bind as demanded

with beeswax or walnut oil
when we had them, or with milk
bought on the way, or flour
and water, or yolks from any nest
I could climb to and rifle—,
though he schooled me in toning
and subtilizing and blending,

and in which roots, shredded
and boiled together, yielded
dark yellows, reds, and blacks—
one morning, aged fourteen, I woke
near Charles Town believing
I could endure my hard paymaster
no longer, without arriving
at fiddlestick's end.

For he wanted my background
oakwoods vague as clouds, my rocks
mere pedestals for his birds,
nothing to draw the eye from his
foreground glories. Unlicked cub
that I was, I could not hold back:

when mud to support his avocet
was called for, I did him an ooze
of modulated umbers and greens
he'd feel between his toes,
payment for all the sloughs I walked
to retrieve whatever life
his aim knocked from the air.

The shadows of my pebbles
lean away from the sun, and every bead's
there in my pod of wild Spanish coffee,
but those plates, inscribed to his patrons,
want the name of the boy
who waded cottonmouth waters
for the swamp snowball
that overwhelms Longabelly's greenlet.

IV

They look but partly hatched
and at a loss about
completing the job, unable
as some men to say if life
goes better outside the egg
or in, and thus, like the half-made
thoughts we live by,
they remain only half-born.
This is one such thought, and I know
if I come to this mud plain
when the creek has taken
itself off, and observe
their clicking and dodging
(and think this thought), I have been
too long about town,
and need a sanative among
the trees. Once in my life
Venus struck me, looked back
across the pubescent
scut of a doe and pointed the mocking
cornu of her ears at me
before graying deeper
into falling snow. She was
a paradigm of you, Mary Colby,
and I followed
the long way home just to see
her footprints untying
and complicating themselves where
water wrinkled around
under ice. Passing the places
where rabbits, mute
until the final moment, struck
exclamations of their emotive lives
on snow, where a squirrel
beat out its terror of being
red on white: Not this! Not me!

in all its skips and evasions,
my great feet effaced everything
but those intimations of her.
When I rowed you
down this water a May evening,
and summoned
a marsh owl for your pleasure,
answering hoot for hoot
as we drifted, the bird
sailing moth-light above the boat,
I knew by your look, beloved
Mary, that you would not have me,
but live as a nun of the frost
or cleave to some thickening cooper
or barrel-counting merchant,
though you had bespelled my spirit
as surely as the blacksnake draws
its quarry from the tree to its
unlatched jaw. Therefore this mud
is hell's floor, that Babel where
the Self lives in its armor,
trotting about, putting itself
in the way, hindering others
with its cutlass-claw. For these crabs
work no more in concert
than feathers in a breeze,
but pluck, pluck, eight-legged
lower natures, mud-colored,
loving the mud, heaping up
middens by their burrows,
scuttering in and out
and sideways like crimps
and flashmen at Horn Fair.
On some that claw attains
size and weight greater than
the body's, as might
the outward sign of some inner
warpage in a man. With this

factotum one gestures
as if offering to extricate a tune
at the drop of a coin. Another
entices a female with it
as it were the season's fashion,
buying and selling, coercing
her down the hole, whilst others
by it are tossed out of burrows
as by crab publicans. They are fierce
to the flesh of drowned
mariners, but when nothing more
than the shadow of a living hand
passes across them, will take in
their eyestalks like spyglasses.
Only here and there on the mudflat
one pauses and seems to meditate,
fumbling as if it may sense
some folly, but discards the thought
and rushes into carnival again.

V

There is one in this country
whom an army cannot make
step to roadside
or increase his pace, which is
commonly no more than
a hand-gallop. For he goes
head-down and teetering,
mincing along like a tall-heeled
trull in his cloud of
rough hair, which can be black
or brown, but is always
whitewashed along the backbone
until the tailtip. He seems of
your polecat species, though
colored more variously,
and of the size of a domestic
cat, but as wide as
he is long. His head is sharp
and snouted like a fop's,
his ears prick up and, belying
his nature, he has eyes
blue-black and childlike, and
is known to promenade
with his family, marching
sire foremost, dame behind,
and kits two and two betwixt,
as in military file.
The Abnakis call him "skunk"
and make large claims
concerning the flavor of
his meat. To stop his forward motion
you merely stamp your foot, but
should he then stamp his own
and begin a backwards shuffle
with tail erect and flirting,
shoot and strike your mark,
lest he spout a liquor on you
yellow as the yolk of an egg,

which can blind for a long hour,
and whose stink, though you wring
yourself hard and sweat
many times to the purpose,
will not disperse.
It is best then to have
business outside the villages,
since you will not sweeten for
a fortnight or more, and must travel
within an effluence
stronger than the halitus
of ten foxes. Nor need you fear
trouble from farmyard dogs or wild beasts,
who will know of your approach
hours before you arrive.
Horses so bespattered run over fences,
rocks, and steeps to roll
in water for hours altogether;
cows in such condition
stand afield unmilked and crying
for the butcher, who will not
come nigh. These skunks
snout around for grubs, beetles,
ant hills and all eggs,
so the ground is funneled
as if a drove of swine has passed,
and by night have been known
to enter houses and with ready teeth
to gnaw through powdering tubs
after the meat, whereat the inhabitants
must look without protest
lest they be spewed on.
The engine of this trouble is
a cistus or bladder holding near
half a pint, and which can be emptied
in a single squirt. I am told
that this organ, when thrown into a fire,
cracks like a musket shot but doesn't

stink. It can be obtained when
the skunk drowns in a muskrat trap,
and thus I have despatched
an agreeable Indian to provide one,
which once in hand I will ship
across the water for you.
For even in the fallen skunk
has the Creator provided
the means for his raising up.
This poisonous stuff, which is
capable of rendering a man
eight hours senseless, will later
revive the heart and work
excellent feats in cheering
the spirit, and being a powerful
ophthalmic, so enriches the eyes
when they're anointed,
that without spectacles the smallest
print may be read.
Taken inwardly or sniffed outwardly,
it cures fits, and disperses megrims
and vertigoes. When you
smell this ordure many days together,
and do not come at the reason
in discovering your corn and
hay crops ruined,
then look to the trees,
where for certain will roost
a horned owl stymied as to night or day
when he stooped
upon this delicate fellow.

VI
(A NEW SECT)

These Passionaries, as you may know,
like to lie about in their finery
and lament their condition. It is nothing
to pass a harmless bush in the country
and have it begin shaking as if
it would burst afire. Formerly you
thought some beast was making its way
through, but now more likely it's
a wretch uttering truisms ready-made
for the tablets. The air fills, all
exclamations and lamentatious vowels,
all ohs! and ahs! mingled,
a catalogue of the believer's crimes
and the most unseemly parts of
his biography. A sort of high holy day
falls sometime in the mud season,
when the March air's pine-chilled,
suffused with water, and the whole cult
leaps from hummock to hummock of snow
in their best livery, wading streams
that flee the hills from a confluence
of snowmelt dropping off a ledge.
Not one of those watery bell pulls,
either, but such a curtain
as would shrink you back to your
proper significance. They enter
that roar through damp ferns and
smoking snow and take a furious dousing.
Wings of it burst up on their shoulders
and the whites of their skulls show
where it beats down their hair.
Then begins a general confession of
failure and shortcomings, as from
a collection of drowned gargoyles.
Shaky songs splatter out of them,
and glossal nonsense, while columns

rush out their sleeves, and shoes
overflow. It beats the stockings
to their very ankles, which, by the time
they are rescued, have turned quite
blue. As for me, I find a quiet walk
across a field in seed salubrious for
shaking off encumbrances
men load upon themselves. It is useful
to stir up a flight of thin, light
membranes, which climb to the air
and are carried to other regions,
there to colonize themselves anew,
or to kick up a dust and arrive
at the far side with pollinated ankles,
gold rings which are not manacles.

VII

If shipboard rats
haven't worried this little beauty
out of condition entirely,
and it has escaped those meddlesome
sorts of sailors who jimmy shipments
with a nose for liquors preserving
specimens, you will see here
a thing which in your old world
has no counterpart. These sleep
all winter, though none among
the Wampanoags can tell me where.
In summer, when I myself so love
to nap in the influence of flowers,
I have been roused by a sudden
buzzy agitation in the bell of
a trumpetvine. At first nothing
is there, then one of these
flower birds, or bird flowers—
they are so ornamented—will fly
backwards out, as quick in
reverse motion as forward,
for they go up, down, sideways
and continuous, and can stand
upon air with only a minor arousal
of it, then brief and direct as
a shooting star proceed to
a grass-pink or trillium to siphon
fragrance through their tubular beaks,
thence perhaps to the lips
of the red turtlehead blossom.
I conclude that they live solely
upon these aromas, favoring
oranges and reds because their vapors
produce the most energy. You will
not be surprised to discover that
I have tried this airy diet myself,
and for days have gone about
without other sustenance, intruding

my nose in blooms, sniffing essences,
careful not to seal the exit of a bee
or whatever else, until my rebellious
appetite drove me to clean out
the cupboard. But would I could drive
the bung home on those fellows
in your country who pronounce upon
our stingy air and unfruitful weathers—
for here's a bird that thrives
upon them! Their own sky is but
a ceiling ringed with painted nymphs,
and could I drop one of those
shrimplings overboard, just as
a great ray is passing, its breadth
that of two gentlemen's cloaks,
it wouldn't fail to elevate
the hairs along his wretched neck.
Or if I could discover the means
of sending across to you a living moose,
its rack like a tree and so plattered
a banquet could be set upon it.
A herd of your deer could cavort
beneath its legs, and posed before it
you would make no more effect than
milady's lapdog. It is true we have
no ruins, no cathedrals, but therefore
no weight of history to wrestle
as a farmer his pasture stones,
only mountains that heave like ocean,
as fit as Sinai for receipt of
prophecy, sublime for the unfolding
of immortality, and waters upon
the landscape equal to a clear eye
in an honest face, and trees which,
were they men, would be grand
originals, models for busts
and frescoes worthy of log houses.
The specious politeness of your

enervated world we are without,
and its disguises. Would we cringe
like toads, our backs mimicking
leaves spotted with decay, not to
offend or disturb? Who meets
an American meets him square-toed,
square-faced in open air, nose out,
the prow of his countenance
broached to whatever weather.
But I am straying from my path again.
The scarlet wimple on the throat
of this bird seems black
in weak light. Other times it passes
through changes that emulate
the tinctures of those flowers it
loves best. I have watched
a female collecting milkweed silk
and down of ferns, saddling them
to an underleaf branch with stolen
spider web and the strings of
caterpillars, then implanting
this device with tree moss.
Hence the nest which I enclose,
its cup formed when the industrious
bird works her body down, fitting it
to the central mass, forming the cup
preparatory for these two eggs
or twin white beans, which are merely
seeds, perhaps more secret in
their processes, but led by the same
warmth and moisture to similar
increase of life. Mantises,
dragonflies, frogs, even
the gummy spider web are this humbird's
nemeses, though one of these
flying fractions will drive after
a crow with the persistence of
a winged auger. An early frost, too,

will stun them from the air
before they can make for winter sleep,
whereby I go about among the trees
collecting them like fruit.

VIII

As to your questioning Mr. Spragg's
whereabouts, he is here, but
in such straits as I would rather
have the hoopsnake's company,
which is said to take tail in mouth
and pursue its prey like an
ungoverned wheel, or the windigo's,
whose prints the size of barrel-mouths
I may have found dripping blood
across snow once. I hazard that
my townsmen will one day
burn Mr. Spragg out, or lead him
to the gallows, for already
they mumble necromancy against him,
and surely he is a man of skill
whose art has outrun sense,
so steeped is he in the hidden
virtues of herbs, from disappearances
among the interior tribes.
He is said to crush and smoke
dried James Town weed, wild lettuce
and wicopy in a sachem's pipe. Even
were he to bring the philtre
that would draw my Mary Colby back
and bid her lay the bundling board
on my fire and undo herself,
that there be no palpable thing
between her whiteness
and my own, I would dread his daylight
approach, draped as he goes
with a string of asarum, St. Andrew's root,
and those large, white, spongy roots
he gathers in the marshes
but will not name, or reveal
the character of. More than once
he has calmed my aching teeth with
the bark of pellitory, but latterly
he has taken himself to the dunes,

his dwelling filched of sea salvage,
away from the talk of sortilege and poisons,
and perhaps from long staring at the blues
and greens in his drift fire, sees things.
Here, as close as I can construe it,
is such a tale, one of his many:
"Of an evening I felt the old beams
dislodging from my house and sliding
seaward, finding their rightful
places in keels and stems. The drowned
fleets came home from Lofoten's Sea
and Nova Zembla, and loomed in that
sober light over the Bars, forms melting
into each other and passing through
without a mast-crack. Barely a ripple,
then they all came up shaking water
off the decks, shuddering amazed at their
new swimming, and lay off there till
the deepening of the morning star."
I attribute such visions in part
to his diet, for he looks upon all the world
as fodder, and would rather assay
the brains of a partridge than her breast meat.
The panther, he assures me, broils to
a savory competing with fresh pork,
and field mice in a batter eat like ricebirds.
The red berry of creeping poxdicaria
he brews to a tea scented cherry-like,
and accounts it a great catholicon
for ridding the body of dropsies.
Nor does he hesitate to try juices of
plants, as the tulip tree, and his walls
are hung with stalks, leaves and flowers,
drying downward. Everywhere in cloth
or birchbark packets, unmarked,
are medicines. Wings of skatefish
and others the sea tosses up
supplement his foodstuffs, and once,

when I feared him frozen to his floor,
so long I hadn't spied him about town,
I went there and he drew for me
what a beach lark spoke to him
out by Peaked Hill that morning.

IX

Mohawk corn refuses no ground:
one grain's sowing in May
means three ears ripe by
October, each of thirty grains
to a row and eighteen rows to an ear,
the planter reaping, like Isaac,
a thousandfold. This lesson is lost
to Jackman, who smears his long face
with berries of mechoacan—a dye
deeper than cochineal—the more
to appear frightening.
His beard is plaited in narrow tails
reaching to his belt, which is
tucked with pistols and daggers.
Hemp cords dipped in saltpeter
he weaves into his hair, and lit
they begin to smoulder.

Jackman steps from the trees
along my path, and scatters
my sketches of broom crowberry
through the forest. He laughs
through wreaths of smoke
as if over some tiresome duty,
then upends my pack,
kicking the seeds around,
dropping sacks in the creek,
grinding the hairy-capped acorns
of red oak under his heels.
These are a mast superior for hogs.
The leaves of its tree,
broad as those of cabbages,
would be alluring to British cattle,
firming and seasoning their flesh
better than anything growing on
your commons, its timber commodious
for houses, fencing, and charcoal.

Hemlock cones he crushes,
a wood hardy as brass for
wharfing, wells and keels,
and strews seeds of that iron tree
which sinks like stone
and may be the anchorwood the Chinese
moor ships with, firing my speculation
that the Western Sea makes inroads
on the farther shores of these
countries, perhaps nearer than we know
if this tree thrives there.
Axes and saws mark the iron tree
no deeper than a grassblade's width
before surrendering their edges,
but only persevere and you have material
for bowls and dishes
which will not crack or break.

Jackman has forsworn such
determinations, and enlisted himself
in that world of night
the savages inhabit. For he eats
from the kettle at their smoky fires,
and wipes fingers greased with
their bear meat, fish, and fat
on his hair and clothes or any passing dog.
His belly and nether organs
he takes for conscience, his only
husbandry the children
randomly-bred upon their girls.

What I now send you I had
stored at home, in camphor-filled jars
to deter the mice,
in snuffboxes and gourds I varnished
against spoiling airs,
and the larger nuts and acorns

dipped in wax. Much I might have conveyed
must await further shipments.

These are but a flea-nip of all to come
from this seed-gatherer's chandlery,
but you must lift your
end of our burden by procuring me friends
who'll support my narrow searches,
for I have gone shank's nag
high and low in these countries,
since many spontaneous shrubs,
growing no taller than my ankle,
I cannot meet closely
on horseback, and my feet often
cry out against me, saying a time will come
when I must refuse to open my pack
until I can sell some of its contents.

Mr. Spragg relates existence of a berry
said to cure swoonings
and melancholy, to clarify heart
and head and bring a man
to livelier conditions upon
chewing six or twelve. These
would be beneficial in my encounters
with Jackman and others.
Not a word passed, as usual,
between him and me, as though
want of usage or his new appetites
have robbed him of speech,
and I live yet because nothing
I own is worth his thieving.
Like many here, he has stumbled
in pursuit of his own lights,
but farther than some.

There's no general remorse about firing
the woods to clear for grains,
root vegetables, and potatoes,

and this completed, since there's
no king in Israel, they resort to
angling, hunting, and drinking spirits
as though bidden to it in Scripture.
Where once a vessel standing
off these shores was embalmed
by the flowering land,
smoke some days clouds the sky
so you might think God's anger is
on the country. Torpid in plenty's
face, the people let pines
bleed quite to death
rather than stanch their incisions
to preserve the matchless turpentine.
So will they flock like sharks to
flawless, dead-straight ones, which are
taken by thousands and sold to mast
the navies of France, Spain, and Portugal,
as their resins ease friction in
the grain and are supplest for dire
weathers at sea. Greater than theft
and murder is counted the crime
of loyalty here, though hemp is plentiful
and so strong that a thread
will slice a finger to the bone.
These traitors and fellows like Jackman
would be repaid by a dance
from it, without benefit of floor.

That is my wicked thought
as I pick myself up and gather
shreds of my person and property
when his appalling laughter
has faded deep enough into the leaves.
I consider I am held in
better regard by those
whose beaded and feathered ways
Jackman's adopted, along with

their risk of starvation
when the snows drive from
the northwest. For they read
in my occupations a form of wizardry,
and leave me to myself.

X

(SOME ENTERTAINMENTS SENT WITH
A GIFT SNUFFBOX CARVED FROM AN
ALLIGATOR'S TOOTH)

I pray this will open prime conversations
for you, and unlock certain minds
across the water. For the alligator
truly is the length of two or three men
from its head, domed like the elephant's,
to the tail, which is flattened
rudderly and as long again
as the body it depends from, and motile
four days when severed. In water
this torso appears first as clusters
of mud, as though the beast were
born of it. But on land it is
mounted on legs like the great tortoise's,
and is horse-thick yet limber and barbed
as a two-man saw. Plated from nape
to tail-tip, it appears hacked
from the stuff of infernal regions.
My first alligator I dragged out of
a fish hawk's grasp when it was
no longer than my foot,
and trained it up on crabs and herring,
until what I hesitate to call gratitude
appeared and strengthened in its nature
at last, and I could with patience
inure it to reins and a light saddle.
After many preliminaries, I galloped
my alligator about the yard
by throwing fishes before it, overlooking
those jaws as long as my arms,
which belch blood when it ramps among
its victuals, though I soon
knew that method would not carry me far.
One morning I glimpsed a better way,
and cast out a living goose tied
to a sapling. We were off down

the Jericho road. Horses dumped
their riders and plunged into brush
to avoid that hysterical fowl
fleeing my land sharkfish, which
the Woccons named Toothed-for-Woe.
Me they called *Monwittetan-Wintsohore,*
Alligator Man, for the way my dragon,
inflating itself, squalled so it leveled
a town of the frowardest savages,
pitching their dogs like bowls on a green.
Later I rode it down the Long River
to the shores of that farther ocean,
where it led me to the cask of some
sea robbers, guarded by headless crows,
and showed me the tree-walled meadow
where I heard the woolly mammoth
bellow and stamp, and witnessed its
sweep of tusk and a strangle of
loosestrife in its great trunk.
Such tales as these I might have indited
nolens volens for the greenhorns of London,
who call the beaver a woodchuck, the woodchuck
a muskrat, adventures to fatten myself
and the plagiarists with while I sat
at my fire thirty years, apiss in tea.
But why the upwelling of pity when I see
one of these slough dogs floating becalmed
or rearing its loaf of a head
and lamenting so hotly that steam issues?
Because those eye-slits and terrible
joineries evince unpurgeable sorrow—
as though it remembered its connivance
and was yet flattened beneath the foot of God?

XI

In positing my earlier theory
I may have been amiss, and therefore
approve your silence upon it,
since not from countless nights
keeping a reed's stillness
among reeds as the day's warmth
climbed visibly out of streams
and the cold slipped into
my bones, so calcifying my feet
that they could be snapped
like parsnips, can I confirm
the heron's power of making
an *ignis fatuus* of its breast down
for enticing its prey after dark,
lit perhaps—as I earlier proposed—
by some phosphorescent
skill drawn from a diet of fish,
or else from a capacity for
storing small electrical charges
it absorbs from water. These ambitions
for discovery may well prove
fatal, as when, recently,
rousing myself from a study of those
loitering April waters
that border paths and roads,
I felt the air draw tight about me,
and what had been distant thunder
sounded nearer at hand, as though
cliffs were cracking off
and sliding from cloud down
to cloud up there. Then in rain
the air was ajump with tap roots
of lightning. Whole systems
flashed between sky and earth,
and bedrock leapt beneath my feet.
I dared not move, for as in that moment
when the bear rises among
the blueberries and attends you,

do you run or hold ground, or take
to the nearest tree? Choose
your authority, though having seen
where lightning moled beneath the earth
and dashed an oak to kindling,
I kept to the one spot, reasoning
that I would visit more points
of entry for those charges
if I rushed about. The quick,
whipping cloudburst done,
and soaked to the marrow, I looked
where sunset now spilled hues
no mortal painter could mix:
bird-yellows, tincture of
mullein-flower, still others of such
delicacy one would discover them
only on the eggs of mallard
and grass finch, perhaps
peregrine falcon and hooping swan.
But read on, Sir, forgiving my divagations
when the point in course arrives.
With the snuffing of that light
came a deep, spring-evening green,
and among titmice and blackbirds
speaking from the marshes,
one at a time petitioning sleep,
arose the needier beseechments
of male frogs. Then, without notice,
almost at each step, I was leapt against
by something, which soon I discerned
to be more frogs. Hundreds,
dropulous with eggs and heading
blindly for those waters. They were rugose
to the touch, their red eardrums
and black lateral stripes lit
by the moon. They plopped
like wet, ocellated sacs,
their ringed eyes bulging from cranial knobs,

straining as if to leap across
some gulf. Long after I gained
higher ground their ructions and snorting
continued, driven as I suppose
by that lightning's influence, which
broke them from their muddy
hibernaculum. Tell me your thoughts
upon this matter. Your interest in
things electrical I know,
and would gladly, should you sponsor it,
present my hypothesis to the Royal Society
in writing: for if that golden farina
which dusts the waters
after spring showers is truly
brimstone the thunder makes, so much
it resembles and reeks of sulphur,
is it not possible that such electric
pulses awaken the season, startle
seeds and open buds and set off
those watery copulations?

XII

I do not believe, as some here,
that the Finns of this region
make storms with their
supposed witchcraft, for they
seem a mild enough, blond people.
Weather will not be charmed,
though clearing the forests
for planting may somehow
ignite changes. Nor do I mean
to include in our ways of
prognosticating such homely
signs as the night arrival of geese
over newly-open water in
February, which yearly disturbs
an old wound under my heart,
for that is simple fact. Patches
my hound has better lore in his nose
than I in my whole frame,
for he takes the morning in,
and knows what wife is peeling
apples, and where, fields away,
the remains of a herring
breakfast may be had.
So complain my townsmen,
who drive him daily from their middens,
his path there from my door
proof enough. Perhaps he inhales,
too, news of the tide's level
at any hour, but here my
reasoning needs factual ballast.
Rain is certain when he turns
on himself more than thrice
before settling at my fire.
So too with Bramber my cat,
whom I might have called
Barometer, for the animals
feel without obstruction
what weathers will arise beyond

our scant horizons, since they
don't afflict themselves with
vanities. When she washes her face
and lies back to the fire,
next day is wet. So too
when the toad is seen at dusk,
or my chimney smoke is a column,
or spreads in this valley
without departing. My bones
do not sense rain at these times,
but I listen for crackling joints
in my chairs and table: the wisdom
pine collected from years in the air.
Each morning I consult red flowers
of the poor man's weathercock,
whose faces being open,
that day goes fair; when closed,
then otherwise. Though there be
many more, here I relate sundry
useful weather saws I have rhymed
to ease my faulty memory:

When Mistress Moon queens
in her horned crown,
the sun grins
and no rain comes down,
but when she dons
her white halo,
snow's to come,
all in a blow.

Seven stars caught in her ring
seven days the storm's a-brewing.

🌲🌲🌲

Spider rings her net up tight,
rain by evening, rain all night.

🌲🌲🌲

Pill-willets low above islands at dawning,
rain before dark, winds lift without warning.

❦❦❦

Six weeks before the frost will fall
the first katydid comes to call.

❦❦❦

Hornet, corn, acorn,
three things betide
hard winters. Nest
of the first
thickened, thickened
husk of the second,
prodigal crop of the last.

XIII
(A NEW-WORLD DREAM)

Nothing had ever fallen
from that sky.
Its sole angels the frigatebirds
rose outspread, feeling for lifting
motions in the air,
or anchored solitary
against the backdrop ocean clouds
which foamed and climbed
unending heights that promised everything.

Below, in a jam of masts and tackle,
men fetched the New World's
bursary aboard. As in a smashed
recessional, some dragged
the alligators, their white
dead bellies up
like those of Gin Lane tosspots.
Deer sprung from life were draped
about shoulders, and tuft-eared
spotted cats, bewhiskered,
heartsore, were hurried leashed
up gangways, and clattering armadillos.

The opossum's young
clutched her fur in terror of red
Narragansetts and Tuskeruros
whose chains rang among
braces of waterfowl: bullnecks
and black-headed whistlers,
runners, flusterers and sea pies.

Then tuns of drumming pearmains
and leathercoat apples,
hurtberries, even king crickets and butterflies
in woven cages. The while
a botany I did not know
whispered from bales and panniers,
species the years might hand down

to me, as ladystem, marsh eelplume,
the common wingtip,
and seamary, mat oakbur,
sheep-ear and eulalia, all I might yet
uncover in my foraging,
even *Erigeron newcombia,*
which I heard on the edge of waking,
and knew I wouldn't live to see
if I kept up my pilfering
this New World for the Old.

XIV
(ENVOY)

I set out
to taste of those thousands
the peddlers gloried over,
apples they said
were strawberries to the nostrils
but sour in the eating,
or hinted of fennel,
or were best at the moment
when green
pales to yellow on the skin,
or the seeds darken,
or the natural waxes surface—
meaning October, when sun
relents and the fruit is racy,
stained with September evenings,
already rusted by fogs, or hangs
purple as ram's horn
where a seed
dropped in an ox turd
took its chances,
sprouted stubborn with thorns
in a far pasture corner, the buds
partridge-trimmed until
there shoved from a juicy
reservoir the one true scion.
I passed up new-grafted whips
for old trees fighting through
lichen and scale—ones
the deer beat a path to
by nose alone—and ate
off the knife from fonts of earth
returning to earth, savoring
local names: the Flavin Surprise,
the Cheek-in-Bloom. You,
in your century, will have
Red Delicious, Granny Smiths,
and a few other perfections

for the eye, but mush
on the palate, cores a dog
rejects by ear for their
want of snap. They will be
fenced against wanderers
like me, and warehoused away,
gassed atrocities, waxwork
celebrities, but no Oneida
Sheepnose or Wethersfield
Beauty, no Garrett's Christmas
Revenge, nothing that has a story
with it, nothing to resurrect
papillae on the tongue
like that apple I found
in a wheelrut once, browned
by November frost,
and thawed in my pocket
and robbed of such wine
the northern lights swam in my eyes.

Winter Oysters (1983)

The Mockingbird

Far into moonlight he tries
to recall his own song,
but a whippoorwill
floats out three notes
wobbly and clear as bubbles,
so he corrects them for her,
melding them with a child's
creaky swing, but erases
that line, and takes a new tack
from a siren on route 17,
then drops to a cowbird
like water poured into water.

This business of getting
the world right
isn't for dilettantes; when
the voices fill you,
you must say nothing wrong,
but follow them back
through the day, going phrase
by phrase over hills,

pausing here and there on a pole
to help goldfinches chip
the sun to a perfect wheel,
dropping by underleaf stones
to improve on mandalas
a cricket's printing in air,
and waiting at cedar posts
to teach killdeer
to pronounce their own names better.

You must bring it all back
alive as the repertoire
of your inner ear,
past fences and over stones,
through one face of leaves
and another
to someone awake on the outskirts,

this woman propped on a pillow,
beginning to see, among fifes,
in her darkened room,
a band dressed like Blue Caballeros.

You must help her imagine
sun living on brass horns,
and an easy, foot-saving march
as the ensemble passes,
air in its wake
banged to a bass difference.

Transmigration

When your bones turn
loose and light as a deck chair
and you raise a rickety
blue pavilion over yourself,

beginning to see from above
how a breeze
ignites marsh grass every-which-way
to new greens,

at first fear will set you down
in the tip of an oak,
your new feet gripping.
Wait. Let instinct assure you
you look like only another
piece of sky between ragged trees.

So this is it.
Who would believe,
this late, this century. . . .

You were running the low tide—
a man in midlife
trying to shake off a pelt
built of too many
trips to too many troughs,
rightly accusing yourself
of having sat out easy rains.

Printing the glacial till
back of Egg Island,
threading pincer movements
of tide, making gulls thrash
water to light, you were
changed in a battering
wink of their wing-storm.

Put everything away.
As if this tree could suddenly
haul in branches and leaves,

you can take in your new wings,
becoming all trunk,
a long-necked sapling
up to the sun.

Then one white stump-crouch
and spring, arms wagging
a quick blue semaphore,
going away until, flat out on air,
that looseness again,
the lattice of bones sliding
above sinews of creeks.

What are you, a soul?
It seems easy to push
earth off and be a diver
exempt from gravity, to flap out
above hay wastes and revolve till
the airport runway could be
a dropped paperclip,

or to glide, a shadow across
hogbacks, for the first time
seeing the art of tractors,
and ocean at practice whittling sandspits,
piling silt like reflected cumulus.

And those ponds back of town,
stations of glacial water
worked by an underworld of
shifting twilights,
permanently cold because
they were shed from the icecap's
orphaned bergs: Little Duck,

a mirage through pines,
where you found the wild wintergreen
and kept a leaf on your tongue,
wishing for deer all the way
to its white shore,

and Ryder, whose beach
you curled up on with one summer's girl
long ago, and woke to Billy Morna,
Old Man Newcomb, the whole road crew
staring over the bank
like kids around a barrel of strange fish—

though such memories are useless,
you find you can go there
and stand in the pale bole
of this new shape, indulging
your hunger for swimming food.

And when blue hollows
invite deeper blues, and marsh
takes on the aura of
undersea fields, last light
drops off the planet's
easy curve, though you rise
in juddering bones to keep it.

What's this? A voice up here?
Voices. Crackles of speech
as off a police radio,
some river of air alive with rage
tearing itself to froth.
Industrial sump, guggle of
money talk shot through
the redolence of a barbecue.

As you pass through the vowels
of love, scenting flowers
whose names, now, you will
never get straight, you know
you will come here often
for snatches of the inconsequential
that bind person to person
and day to day below,

where Main Street seems to be lifting
moonward, and headlights run
out a few capillary roads
among dunes grained
like the surface of old bones.
Veering, you scout for
a sour updraft of pond.

And in the end, come to yourself
above roofs struggling unequally
out of leaves. Hearing bells
crosscut by rifts of wind,
and an organ thin as a harmonica.

Lifted from that pattern
you can't feel for what you trail
above familiar cars up Main Street,
Commercial, School Street,
arriving over Memorial Lawn,

and nothing you could say
to that veiled woman
and downcast kids would explain
this simple rightness of things.

The wind shifts, and as if
in a time lapse, maples begin
flaunting their reds. Arranging
the town off one wing, and sea,
squalling up, off the other,

you hang out on air until
white, blue white, yellow,
the cloud-pelted moon
drags up new stars, magnitudes
winking out of the portside dark.

A Double-Ended Dory

You may never understand
why I shoveled the zinnias out of her
after closing time, looking over
my shoulder for cops, if you've
never put offshore
in anything but a hull like tupperware.
But she sat out the calm
in front of the Chowder House,
a hangdog flower bed
sad as a purebred pointer
wearing a Christmas bow.
Her gunnels were hand-shaved,
her strakes had been soaked to fitting
curves, and when I dug out
her ribs and knees, they still evoked
arches and buttresses. Once she was
tight as a pod, clinker-built
for cod-lining on the Banks:
the deeper the fish in her bins,
the surer she sat two men
in the troughs between waves.
Remembering coves where her corners
might still hold rain
and a plankton swirl, I got one end
up on the tailgate, then shoved
feeling hope throw its weight in
with mine, and took the old county road.

Winter Oysters
Ellen's poem

February: water and sky a gape
hinged at Great Island,
mudflats and cottages scoured
of summer, but a few car trunks
open to wire buckets and rakes
with serious teeth, and a few
aficionados of wind
sliding thick socks into waders
and hooking up, ready under hoods
and watch caps to break through
the tideline's rime, later
to break with short, upturned blades
into shells parted from rocks
and "dead man's fingers." This
is how we like them, not summer-thin
and weepy tourist fare, but hale
as innkeepers, their liquor clear,
fat with plankton that thrives
under a glaze drifting just below
green water, and without any
lemon sundrip or condiment
but a dash of bourbon to punctuate
each salty imperative.

Dog Love

Now the shadow of the wolf in him
wakes early. Before even a hairline of light
he paces the house, whining the sting
of each love dart till I wake
and begin weighing him with human analogies.
I know this wallowing in the soup of self,
that alphabet spelling me, me,
my insides flapping like a love-struck leaf,
all sense loping off on the heels
of every urge. When I unlock the dark
he goes straight for the woodpile
where the little bitch has set up
housekeeping. And he has unlocked
something I thought dead, the puritan
only sleeping in me: I could keep him
from kibble and scraps just to test
which hunger is stronger.

In the light rain before coffee
I whistle him back, but only part way,
relearning "hangdog" by the wet drape
of his ears. When he looks with concern
to the stacked wood, I hear the tearing
of our treaty, and meditate on guilt
and conditioning when he gives me a profile
but won't look me in the eye.
Will he seem older when she runs him off
snapping at his tendons, who has lured him
with love nips about the face?
She is not the one I would have chosen
for him, and at first, given her size,
I doubted the feasibility of it all.
But now I wonder if it's hot water
or cold you douse them with
before the schoolbus comes.

Atlantic Flyway (1980)

Young Owls

Now crows mill blackly above them,
yawking as though
something is stuck in their craws,
and a panic of baby white
floats off the nest as if
struck in midflight.

But they are there,
trying deficient wings
and feet like goalies' mitts
at the nest's brink,
trying a gargle of little bones
and a stare like corpse candles,
their black pupils fixed in yellow.

They sit it out,
or lean into the future,
waiting for their buff feathers
to straggle downhill through scrub
till they are dressed like bark.

Visitations of neither
luck nor wisdom, they mean
no frogs in the garden this year,
no hunting the slope under the nest
for lady slippers
languorous with spring.

Dropping to berry tangles
on feet that later, quicker,
will snatch June bugs from the air
and flip them like popcorn
to their beaks,
they waddle toward dusk

and clutches of young terns
in the hollows on Egg Island,
fuzzy about how shadows
drop out of the sun,
how nothing in this world
gets out of its life alive.

1847

1: *A Man from Adare, County Limerick*

> *Halfway down Constitution Hill the report of a pistol was heard.*
> *. . . Queen Victoria stood up, and said to the page accompanying*
> *her, "Renwick, what was that?" "Your Majesty has been shot at,"*
> *replied Renwick.*

It wasn't loaded, or else
loaded wrong, and the man
from Adare was mentally
deficient, maybe
from boiling nettles behind
a bush or begging from inside
a hollow tree while his family
flapped in rags across a field,
hopping barefoot, hunting
row to frozen row
for one glabrous turnip.

Maybe he'd just been skinned
by a passage broker in Liverpool,
and a crimp ran off with
his sea chest while mancatchers
on each arm were trying to pull him
two ways to innkeepers.

Shoveled out, improved off the land,
too poor to be ballast for
a Black Star packet, his fate in
the failed potato, maybe he survived
the season of blackberries
while his children stared
like storybook rabbits
from under a scalpeen: his own
walls thrown on a ditch by
crowbar brigades, the landlord's
payment for rent owed.

Sir Robert Peel has a smile
like the silver plate on a coffin.

Indian corn is his brimstone,
and pokes through a child's
belly like nails through a sack.
When he laughs it's time
to finish the raw cabbage
and start on the seaweed, it's time
for the Dearth and Scarcity Prayer,
for black leg and black fever,
jaundice and the bloody flux,
road fever and typhus.

If Your Majesty pressed her palm
to the hollow of this updrawn
shoulder blade. . . . Heaven tugs
on invisible wings while Hell
drags at the heels,
but there's no tear, only the stare
and muslin pallor, the senile
gape of the man from Limerick's
bald, bearded daughter.

2: *Report of the Board of Potato Commissioners*

If, because of static electricity
generated by locomotive effluents,
or the mortiferous vapours of
blind volcanoes beneath the earth,
or from the guano of sea fowl
or the potato dropsy or other causes,
your crop is diseased, avail yourself
of a rasp, one square of linen cloth,
one hair sieve or cloth strainer,
two tubs of water and a griddle.
Now grate the unspoiled crop finely
into a tub, wash, strain,
again wash and strain, then dry
resulting pulp on griddle over
slack fire. Milky starch

precipitated in wash water, when
mixed with the dried pulp
of peas-meal, oatmeal, or flour,
makes wholesome bread or
farinaceous spoon meat. Sliced
potatoes soaked in bog water or
oven dried, or spread with lime
and salt, or treated with a mixture
of vitriol, MnO_2, and salt—
said mixture producing chlorine gas—
or baked 18–22 minutes on your cabin fire
at 180° F. . . . All true Irishmen,
we are confident, will exert themselves
to all we recommend, though
there may be a deal of trial and error
at first. If you don't understand
these directions, consult your priest
or landlord.

3: *Steerage*

If you could set stones on the Atlantic
from Liverpool to Grosse Isle
or New York, some would have graves.

In steerage the luckiest girl
got wedged between her brothers,
and lived despite Holloway's Pills
reputed to cure twenty-three things
worse than the Earl of Aldborough's liver.

Born unlucky, some slipped overboard
weighted with shot and unshriven,
taken by ship's fever
or water bunged in old sperm oil casks.

An orphan could get a customized name
in New York, and One-eyed Daley's
ticket for Detroit could end him
in Albany forever.

Grosse Isle seems to float
its white chapel and fever sheds
on a green shimmer in the St. Lawrence.
Everywhere you step
into the indentations under grass.

Old Map of Barnstable County

It doesn't show
how the cold edge of starlight
pierced woodpiles,

or the boy forking hay
who one afternoon cries out to no one
on the shore of Still Pond
and runs away to sea,

but crawls ashore years later,
to lie under this mapmaker's
pinpoint, which stands for "humane house,"
and gasp white-eyed on the straw floor,
his hands scrabbling his chest
for its breath.

Who would believe,
on this mapmaker's Atlantic
which looks safe as a strip of corduroy,
a schooner is floundering,

and soon heartbreak will walk
the sand roads up hollows
to Mrs. Small, Mrs. Snow, Mrs. Dyer,
sea widows whose lives will go on
in ways the cartographer's black squares
for houses can never explain?

A red dot for each vessel lost
would turn this map
to a rash like scarlet fever,

quick as a camera's shutter
that sea would close over islands,

and the griefs that went by the names
beside the black squares
would move on to other squares,

as on later maps
even the black squares
will have moved on.

Pitch Pines

Some trees loft their heads
like symmetrical green bells,
but these, blown one-sided
by winds salted out of the northeast,
seem twisted from the germ.
Not one will lean the same way as another.

Knotted but soft, they mingle
ragged branches and rot to punkwood,
limbs flaking and dying
to ribs, to antlers and spidery twigs,
scaly plates slipping off the trunks.

Hanging on, oaks rattle maroon clusters
against winter. But these, resinous in flues,
blamed for a history of cellar holes,
snap in the cold and fall
to shapes like dragons asleep,

or thin out by dropping sour needles
on acid soil. For one week in May
they pollinate windows, a shower
that curdles water to golden scum.

From Bartholomew Gosnold's deck,
Brereton saw this cape timbered to its shores
with the hardwoods that fell to keels
and ribbing, to single meetinghouse beams
as long as eight men.

Stands of swamp cedar, cleared for cranberries,
were split to shakes or cut lengthwise
for foundations, while sheep cropped
elm and cherry sprouts
and plows broke the cleancut fields.

Fifty cords at a time, birch and maple
melted bog iron in pits; elm and beech
boiled the Atlantic to its salts; red oak
fired the glassworks at Sandwich—

till the desert floundered
out of the backlands and knocked
on the rear doors of towns
and this peninsula drifted
in brushfire haze,

and, clenching their cones
under crown fires, the grandfathers
of these pines held on until
heat popped their seeds
to the charred ground.

Old Old Woman, Little Girl

One is beginning to learn
what the other is forgetting,
one preparing to go
where the other has been,

and they feed each other
from twin kitchen chairs,
the space between
as clear as a sky beyond
two branches, one tapering out,
the second a nub
of everything possible,

while we stand
in the eighty years between,
thumped by abstractions,
in a crossfire of love and money.

Neither is always certain
who the other belongs to,
and with both it's a matter
of how many teeth, of when
to be put to bed,

of sharing the other's spoonful
like a secret withheld from us
because they are nearer
that point on the circle
where questions are useless,

where pleasure is
two voices rising and dropping
branch to branch
for the red berries of delight.

The Trip by Dream Train

Engine and tender, old loaf-shaped Pullman.
I am making the trip alone
because of the house a dream within this dream
keeps erecting in my sleep.

It is always barely April, but at loading docks
behind the church-topped mills, in the cinders
and shattered weeds, it is late November.

No one is on the streets, no one's not working,
and the workday flashing past looks empty,
the storefronts blind. Not one pane of forty-eight
in a factory window winks; just row on row,
banked like the pigeonholes
in a postal clerk's nightmare.

In a side yard a hairless, vested man
rakes among shadows eloquent as the clang
of steel doors. There are joined angles of bridges,
tanks with coolie hats, a distant refinery
like stacked poker chips,

but always that house, white in April sunlight,
nearly perfect except for broken slats
in the green, nailed shutters.

Then the piney backs of towns, and blond fields
where rocks seem to crawl out of their shadows,
and the slow progressions into small, identical
cities of brown bungalows and triple-deckers,
clatter of Redcaps' dollies, arrival and departure

through which I see the shadow of a crow
crossing white shingles in light so clear
it could be bottled and sold.

Switchyards and sidings, men working gears
with levers, municipal power blocks, trestles,
at one stop the illusion of slipping back
when the cars alongside begin to move;

finally the coast, where a tug trundles upriver
and one seabird crosses high and slow,
a hint of prehistory in its flight,

then cranberry bogs, ditch-ruled and crossed
with levees supporting pump houses,
a set of iron wheels stunned in sunlight.

I try to see the roof of that white place,
the red brick chimney's shadow,
the rainstreak of mortar like a second shadow.

Under cirrus brushwork the creeks
crawl into harbors, their soft tides
feeling seaward in various blues, opening out
under sky opening out.

Crossings too small for gates and lanterns blur by,
each with its warning X,
and one by one, joined by railside wires,
minor stations appear on the line,

a country of white houses whose one-story
bedrooms and late ells meet their barns,
whose oil drums sit on sawhorses.

I stop this trip by its pullcord, and step down
to a sooty cream station trimmed in maroon,
a coalbox alongside, and walk up a two-lane road
nothing is moving on.

The light is always April, chilled amber,
the air headier than I imagined.
Beyond the Big Dipper Dancehall, torn
to its baseposts thirty years ago,

I turn onto a sand road, pass cabins shut
till June, and Ed Mather's place;
he elected to live up hollow from everything
but a deer run and weather.

If I find that house where locust trees
shadow the flaking paint,
will I pry its green storm door and break
the frosted pane over the inside knob,

and enter rooms abandoned to mothballs and
mousedirt and that gray matter that springs out
on old shoes, and call that warehouse
of sheeted furniture home?

A Triptych for Snowlight

1.

Are these the same chickadees who rolled
in the wet cabbages
and tracked down June bugs half their size?
Caught like them
between one wind and another
feeling us out
like products each means to buy,
there is just enough time
to relearn the chestnut streaks of
a fox sparrow and
the cardinal's Assyrian beard
before the sun dissolves
in albuminous snowlight.

2.

Now caterpillars of snow
cling to every branch, intending to stay, and wind
begins sneering beneath
eaves and sills.

Is some pale wretch
floundering to her knees out there,
a small bundle of dreams
swaddled in her arms

as the woods tilt a new way
to the chonk and sizzle of ice in the flue,
heaven's crockery
thrown down on our heads?

3.

Motes are jeering.
Pips who razz snow though it tries
to snuff them everywhere
are tugging the light,

even the shy redbird
is tucking light back into place.

On the still life of the mulch,
sun ignites citrus and apple skins,
and a crow puts on
the brow I wore all night
and walks the gangplank of a broken pine.

The Minutes No One Owns (1977)

Glass

What the warbler must have seen
was the world swung round;
without turning back
she was flying into
a distance already passed through:

another side of the woodpile
she had just cleared in a single pitch,
and beyond, through the middle ground
of pines, the background glitter
of running sea she had skipped above
like a flat stone thrown so well
it touches down on water
all the way to the other shore.

Swung round,
only slightly blurred.
Trees twinning,
far water grained,
air of a density . . .

then that split-second insight

into splashes of newspaper
and clothing,
filtered through
final dusts of light.

As perhaps,
in our last seconds,
we are swung round
to live ourselves back through
each particular,
to fall faster and faster
out of loves, out of
changes of clothes,

whole snows lifting skyward
becoming autumn leaves lifting
back into green trees,

the dead stepping out of
crumbling loam,

at the last, seed and egg
unraveling, falling away.

And all
in the time
it takes a flat stone to skip over water
and be let in.

A Photo of Miners

(LEWIS HINE, 1908)

With trees backing them
instead of the pit's mouth,
they could have been
at a fifth-grade picnic.
But the spitballer won't grow into
his father's jacket, and a ladder
of safety pins climbs the front of
the class clown. Stretch,
who got tall the soonest,
has the air of a chimney sweep,
and here is a little grandfather
in brogans and rag gloves,
his face shoved between two shoulders
his arms are draping,
his eyes flashing the riding lights
of pain. They are a year's
supply, average age, give or take
a year: ten. Don't look for
a bare foot at a devil-may-care
angle on one of the rails,
or a habitable face for a life
you might have led—that
mouth is rigid as a mail slot,
the light on those hands predicts
common graves. Does anything transcend
the walleyed patience of beasts,
the artless smirk on the boy
with the high forehead
who thinks he will croon his way
out of this?

The Old Clothes

Often I visit them where they slump
in the closet, hangers protruding
like beggars' shoulder blades.
Splotched as if they'd endured
barrages of fruit, as if the body,
short-circuiting, let go its fluids
and salts, a blowout frazzling cuffs
and throwing off buttons
like a millionaire flinging coins
in his old neighborhood,
I should cram them in a poor box
in some parking lot far from home,
except they'd be back that night,
cowering or stiff as the line-up,
pockets bagged for larceny
or deflated by keyholes, derailed
and toothless zippers, knees
weak as unanswered prayers.
I should pay some crone
to slash up the lot
and hook me a rug for my old age,
something to keep on my lap
and pick up a clue from—
some thread of evidence
that proves I was going straight.

Fear of *Gray's Anatomy*

I will not look in it again.
There the heart in section is a gas mask,
its windows gone, its hoses severed.
The spinal cord is a zipper
& the lower digestive tract
has been squeezed from a tube like toothpaste.
All my life I had hoped someday to own
at least myself, only to find I am
Flood's ligaments, the areola of Mamma,
& the zonule of Zinn. Ruffini's endings
end in me, & the band of Gennari lies near
the island of Reil. Though I am a geography
greater than even I surmised, containing as I do
spaces & systems, promontories & at least
one reservoir, pits, tunnels, crescents,
demilunes & a daughter star, how can I celebrate
my incomplete fissures, my hippocampus &
inferior mental processes, my depressions
& internal extremities? I encompass also
ploughshare & gladiolus, iris & wing,
& the bird's nest of my cerebellum,
yet wherever I go I bear the crypts of Lieberkühn,
& among the possible malfunctionaries,
floating ribs & wandering cells, Pott's fracture,
mottles, abductors, lachrymal bones & aberrant ducts.
I will ask my wife to knit a jacket for this book,
& pretend it's a brick doorstop.
I will not open *Gray's Anatomy* again.

Needsong

Sweetmeat, what we need is a tune
scored in bedrock, something
that leaks out of burrows in the grass
& keeps alive one twitch
someplace. We'll both be under
sometime anyway, maybe of something
unmentionable, like intracardial
traduction, with two rich surgeons
still in their twenties
standing over us mumbling
"reverse breach contractor," &
"post-affection decimation ratio."
We've already believed in
so many things that are wrong,
why not one more interlude
for the living, something to sing
when the odor of pears from a bag
sticks us back in the first grade
far from torts & the tarot,
where the sky can look in windows
& see the doorway & our mothers
unknotting our fists from theirs
& nudging us over the oiled floors
toward Miss Stone. O Dark Lady,
remember: the twenty-six letters
you couldn't read & those sullen
janitors downstairs shoveling
into their hives? The baby's
the age my sister was when
the half-moons were drawn
in death's kohl under her eyes
& the blue bows in her hair
couldn't hide her bones being readied
for their flight. This is
a song about ampersands. I know
you've got my troubles & I've
got yours: we need a tune that'll

iron out the whole convolvulus
& settle the scores of worry on our
foreheads, something we can whistle
on the paths among the trees.

No Time for Good Reasons (1974)

The Winter Runner

Then he invented the running wolf behind the wind,
the rifle barrel edged from frozen bushes,
stories for turning sluggish ropes of blood,

reddening the rorschach in his heart's
salt cave. For courage he recalled
the inchworm going home,

high in the glow of summer dusk,
two hundred forty times above itself.
His forehead slicked with dross

of the distilling blood.
He felt his eye roam clear,
drink in the afternoon:

the amber sun, the low hills afterthoughts
between the sea and sky,
ice locked in ringed panes

like the years of trees.
In loose flocks, evening grosbeaks
flung out of the branches,

yellow flags a summer had left over.
Then he was running where
pines dipped their shadows in a sluice

of water. Slowing to walk against the wind
he let slip through his fingers,
as quiet as the time, time entered in:

the orange, thumbnail tip of sun
and last fruits of day: eelgrass softening
from tan to plum:

sky going down on fire
behind an island: the purpling sea:
sky citrus, pear, then empty of these lights.

Long Pond Summer

Dawn creeping gray from offshore
scattered the ducks beelining
across the water.

Each needle bled its pine droplet
of sun and sent squirrels tattering
over the tarpaper roof.

Some mornings
you woke to a dream
of the snout of a wayfaring hound

outside your screen.
A skreak of the cast-iron pump
and from under all Wellfleet

the gurgling of ferrous water rose up
and the day began. Through
the bellicose howls of kids

in love with a sinking float,
you thought of the tired clump
of fur and claw in the road,

and wrote a poem ending in 'strange.' Selling
air-conditioned meat
to bronzed New Jersey matrons,

leaning close you bartered with your lust.
Outside the cicadas sang *heat.*
And in evenings green as apples,

home to the driftwood fire;
in the devil-glare redness of lobster,
a girl slipping off her white sweater,

like the moon coming up on long water.

After Midnight

In Kansas a shadow is moving
across one yellow square
of farmhouse window
into my sleep.
At a line behind his place
the stars leave off
and the earth comes in
from the horizon like a breeze,
keeping his floor and the phone
on his secondhand table
from joining the night
above those stars. In ringing
Connecticut I drop back
to the same earth
at the same time an hour older
and headlights are rolling
over and over like lanterns swung
on the road to Atchison.
Thin as a paper cup, metal quits,
and then, or now,
a woman is bleeding and someone
that might have isn't going to
live. Across 1,500 miles
tires, brake linings, the weave
of a prayer
fray with the recitation
of another year.

Stealing the Christmas Greens

Fifty miles down the road you can give
five bucks to some guy
with a thread-riddled nose
like a road map of Vermont
and get a symmetrical tree.
Not me. Third-growth pine
is best, where sand farmers have failed
and where it was recut
to fire a tryworks in whaling days.
A broken puzzle of snow on the ground,
wear a coat long enough to bootleg in
a saw. This bottom was Ned
McLaughlin's, those mounds
are where he spaded his dead
horses. Look close
and you might see a wicket of ribs
stick up like a rotting skiff.
Now look for a tree
whose northeast side isn't flat
with wind off Georges Bank.
Be sure to top it high and light enough
so you can drag it back. Keep off the roads,
or if you really have to move,
being seen, balance it easily over
one shoulder. It's more than likely
once you set it up you'll see the top
won't point, but forks,
imperfect as a life, no pinnacle
for an angel. A green bow
and a chocolate Santa Claus
dressed in red foil will camouflage
that gray spot on the trunk.
Now plug it in, no talk of ritual,
get out the bourbon (each sip's
Christmas Eve), and rinse a glass clean
for the chief of police.

The Bats

Somebody said for killing one
you got a five-dollar reward
from Red Farrell the game warden,
because at night they drank cow blood,
dozens of them plastered on the cow
like leaves after a rain,
until she dropped.
If they bit you you'd get paralyzed for life,
and they built their nests
in women's hair, secreting goo
so you couldn't pull them out
and had to shave it off.
That was how Margaret Smith got bald,
though some said it was wine.
But who ever saw one
or could tell a bat from the swifts
they sometimes flew with,
homing on insects those green evenings?
We never climbed the fence of Duffy's orchard
to catch them dog-toothed
sucking on his pears,
and the trouble was, as Duffy always said,
that in the dark you couldn't
recognize them for the leaves
and might reach up and get bit.
So the first time one of us found one
dead and held it open,
it looked like something crucified
to a busted umbrella,
the ribbed wings like a crackpot would make
to try and fly off of a dune.
As if it was made up of parts
of different animals, it had long bird-legs
stuck in lizard wrinkle pants,
and wire feet.
It wasn't even black, but brown and furry
with a puppy nose,

and when we threw it at each other
it wouldn't stick on anyone.
Then someone said his father knew somebody
who used to hunt between town and the back shore.
Coming home one night he ran across
a bat tree in the woods,
must have been hundreds folded upside down
pealing their single bell-notes through the dark.